A Quick and
Handy Guide for
Writers,
Webmasters,
eBayers, and
Business People

Web
Content
Rx

By

WAYNE ENGLISH

CAREER
PRESS
Franklin Lakes, NJ

WEB CONTENT RX
EDITED BY KATE HENCHES
TYPESET BY EILEEN MUNSON
Cover design by The Designworks Group
Printed in the U.S.A. by Courier

To order this title, please call toll-free 1-800-CAREER-1 (NJ and Canada: 201-848-0310) to order using VISA or MasterCard, or for further information on books from Career Press.

The Career Press, Inc., 3 Tice Road, PO Box 687,
Franklin Lakes, NJ 07417
www.careerpress.com

Library of Congress Cataloging-in-Publication Data

English, Wayne (Wayne Angelo)
    Web content RX : a quick and handy guide for writers, webmasters, eBayers, and business people / by Wayne English.
        p. cm.
    Includes index.
    ISBN 978-1-60163-068-1
    1. Web sites—Design—Handbooks, manuals, etc. 2. Technical writing—Handbooks, manuals, etc. 3. Visual communication—Handbooks, manuals, etc. I. Title.

TK5105.888.E538 2009
006.7—dc22

2008054109

To my dear wife,
and most severe critic,
Joanne.
Without your support and editing
this book and my life
would not be what they are.
And to
"the best daughter that's ever been," Elizabeth.

Acknowledgments

To my wife, Joanne, for her exhaustive, word-by-word, edit of the manuscript. This book would not be what it is without her efforts.

I am indebted to the staff at Career Press., especially Michael Pye, senior acquisitions editor and director of product development, Kirsten Dalley, editor, and Kate Henches, for her insightful comments and editing.

I would also like to thank my dear friends Mark Coleman, a Flash animation expert, and Chris Boyd, musician, for their kind assistance and friendship. Also Tim Laubacher of Laubacher Multimedia and Matt Service of Service Internet Solutions for allowing me to use their names and products; J. Thomas Wenzel III and the management of Sir Rebel films; Peter Crowley, photographer; and Rob Miller at Host Cabin.

To those kind enough to endorse this book, a most special thank you to, in alphabetical order, Joyce Boncal, Ryan Davis, Stephen Dombeck, and J. Lindsay Kellock.

Contents

Introduction

WebContentRx.com, the business, was formed to meet the growing need for services related to business communications and to make business-related Web sites more effective. So to meet that need:

- ❯ We design, develop, and host Web sites.
- ❯ We research and write keyword-laden Web content.
- ❯ We Search Engine Optimize the content and the Web page(s) that carry the content.
- ❯ We do e-mail marketing.
- ❯ We provide our clients with digital photography.
- ❯ We write and disseminate media releases.
- ❯ Our customer service is fantastic and there is never a charge to chat. We even buy the coffee.

We treat your Web site as we would an employee, with a job to do, a cost to the company, and a benefit to the company. Like any other employee, the site must do its job—else you're throwing your money away.

The Web is no longer the province of scientists, engineers, and those with technical skills. Now the Web is where we shop, hang out, play, buy, sell, and get to know each other. The Web has changed and the needs of those who use the Web have changed. We aim to meet those needs.

In 2009, the quality of the content that businesses and people put on the Web is now recognized as being important. No longer is just cutting and pasting lots and lots of text (fluff) onto a Web site taken as a substitute for substantive content.

From now on content will remain important to the Web as long as the Web is important to people. As an information retrieval and delivery tool, the Web is without equal. The true value, the genius, the very capability of the electronic world is that it is adaptable and able to incorporate new and old ideas. Old ideas? E-mail, the true killer application, was invented in 1971. The Web did not come along until 1980. E-mail fit right in.

So, content and the quality of content have arrived and will remain important for the future, certainly for the life of the Web and then on whatever technology replaces it.

We believe that no discussion of content is complete without including Web code, design, and keywords. To deliver high-quality content that coveys a message and provides the necessary information for search engines is just doing the job and part of the services that anyone paying for a Web site has every right to expect. What's the point of placing great content on the Web if no one can find it? So, a knowledge of Web development will aid you as a writer, make the Web master's job easier, and make the finished product richer. Further, knowing something about the technical side will enhance your value as a wordsmith and increase your income, but, be advised, we will not attempt to make you a Web master. While we clearly include technical material there is no attempt to make you a geek. For those who have technical skills and want to add writing to your resume, you will find the technical material will enhance your skills. What is contained here concerns the writer. It will be a tremendous asset to you personally, professionally, and economically.

So, whether you are a Web master, a technical writer, work in industry, write eBay ads, or just want to put good stuff on your site, we planned and wrote this book for you.

Get Read or Get Lost—
Your Content Decides

> *"Put it to them briefly, so they will read it; clearly, so they will appreciate it; picturesquely, so they will remember it; and, above all, accurately, so they will be guided by its light."*
>
> —Joseph Pulitzer

1

On December 24, 1877, Thomas Edison patented the phonograph. No one ever bought a phonograph. No one ever bought a radio. No one ever bought a television. No one ever bought a video cassette recorder (VCR), a compact disk (CD), or a digital video disk (DVD). No. What they bought was a content delivery system. We start by speaking of Edison because he began the electric march into the future. We could have begun with Gutenberg and the printing press because, you see, it is not the technology that people want, but the content that the technology delivers. It is the content that is important, that is sought, that is bought and paid for.

The Web is no different from a printing press, or a phonograph, or a DVD, or whatever *technology* comes next. What is important is the content that the technology delivers. It is the content that people pay to hear, see, or interact with. It is the content that people want. It is the content that your customers will pay you to create. It is the content that pays for the technology that delivers it.

Think about audio content. It was played live, and only live, for centuries. Then it was recorded. While technology after technology that delivered music has gone obsolete, the music endures. Remember eight-track tape? Probably not; it's obsolete. Remember vinyl albums and 45 RPM records? They're obsolete too, while recorded music is more successful than ever. Just consider the iPod, and the software that runs on computers to play music. The music, the content, is alive and well. While the technology changes, the music endures.

Throughout this book there is one overriding theme. It is that content is important. There are countless examples of content making its way down the ages. From cave drawings, to painted scenes in the pyramids, to perhaps the most successful content delivery system of all time: books. Don't be taken in by the sound of lasers, bells, and electronics as your mouse alights on a link. Don't be fooled by bright flashing colors that supposedly get attention and make you spend money. The messenger is not the message.

The *message* is the message—and the message is the content.

It was always about content and it will always be about content. Content is king. Even when you hear, and read, that content is not king. That is a ruse; read what they have to say. Those who say content is not king quickly add that the user, the reader, is king. In that, your majesty, there is no doubt. Content is the only thing that matters. If you doubt that think of:

» The Bhagavad Gita

» The Bible

» The plays of Shakespeare

» The prophecies of Nostradamus

» The *Art of War*, by Sun Tsu

» The Constitution of the United States

» The Bill of Rights

» Countless other texts that have withstood the test of time

The technology that the content resides on has changed and will continue to change. The content itself will not. It's not the Web that is important; it is the content that the Web delivers. What makes the Web superior are the Internet services that run on it, its ability for interactivity, e-mail, file transfer protocol (FTP), the vast array of audio and video capability, the programming languages and scripting tools that allow for the plethora of material available to people everywhere, and, of course, hypertext links. The Web allows unparalleled communication and the ability to move data quickly and easily. This and high-speed connectivity make the Web a superior environment for the delivery of content. On that, we would never disagree. However, those services are icing on the cake, not the cake itself. Sure, on the Web, you can shop in real time, instant message, and download everything from software to songs, but how did you do those things before the Web existed? You shopped, got information, and listened to music. Is the Web a major step forward? Of course, but the Web also brings the dark side of human experience right into your home, right into your mind, often unbidden. That too, is content, but content that we do not necessarily want. The World Wide Web is quite literally like the Wild West. There are good guys, bad guys, cops and robbers, and just plain folks working and living and wanting nothing more than to raise their children in a safe place. And it is the content running on the Web that helps and hinders all those things. Whether you think it is good content, bad content, protected speech, or vile hate, it's the content that is good or bad.

And, having said all that, as far as we are concerned, content is text because text is what search engines find at least for now and the foreseeable future.

The Web: What It Is and What It's Not

The Web is an information retrieval system. Sure, of course. So what? The Web is not the message. It is the messenger; the Web brings the message. Don't be deceived by all the technological blinking lights, bells, whistles, and technical fanfare. Look close; look hard; see beyond it. Once a teacher of mine told us that you see with the mind, not with your eyes. See what is there; see the message. Is it the message you want to convey? Don't be impressed by all that color and hoop-la. If you do not make sure the user receives the intended message, you're finished. And all the money spent on your site— gone. And your competition wins. No, that's not right. They did not win. You were never serious competition because your message was so bad. You simply lost. Never, ever, be blinded by all that technology. See the message. If you don't, won't, or can't, then *you* are who *I* want to compete with because I won't give you the chance to do things twice.

Search Engines Find Content

Never in human history has so much content been accessible by products that exist only to find something. If you think that because your favorite search engine cannot locate what you are looking for means that it does not exist, you are wrong—so very, very wrong. A search engine sends its robots to scan the Web and bring back data on what is found and the Web address where it was found. No search engine searches the entire World Wide Web when you issue a query. Many people think that a search engine actually does that. Not so. Your query searches only the data available to the search engine in its data warehouse. Keep that in mind next time you can't find what you know is out there. That is why using more than one search engine is a good idea. They do contain different information in their data warehouses. When search engines fail, you hit the books in the library, because not everything is on the Web. Good libraries can't be beat. Research librarians are worth their weight in gold when you need difficult to find information.

There is another reason to be aware of this. You can easily and inexpensively use Google, and other search engines, to provide site search capability for those who visit your Web site. We will talk more about that later. Keep in mind that, for any search engine to find material on your site, that material must have been scanned and its location must exist in the search engine's data warehouse. When you add content to your site, that data is not in the data warehouse until your site, and the new data it contains, are scanned and the information on what it is and where it is gets back and updates the search engine's data warehouse. So be advised that just because you add content to a Web site does not mean that it is instantly able to be found by search engines. It does not work that way.

Here is s feature you may be able to use. Have you ever needed to find something on a Web site that you know is there, but can't find it? That happens all too often. What to do? Use Google to search the site for you. To access this feature select **Advanced Search from Google's main page.** Many search engines offer this feature besides Google. It is a superb tool for finding specific material on huge sites. (Note: Because of the technical differences between databases and directories, we opted for the term *data warehouse(s)* to make the writing and reading easier.)

It is the ability of search engines to index, retrieve, and create hypertext links to content that makes the Web as we know it possible. Can you imagine the Web without search engines? It would be like looking for a leaf in a forest—chaos. The Web would be a morass of disorganized data. Rather than the superb resource that we know and love, the Web would be worthless without search engines because you could not find anything.

While it is true that video, audio, and images can be thought of as content, search engines cannot find them directly, or index their content. It is the associated text that search engines find, read, record, and work with. For the foreseeable future, search engines will remain text-based hunter-gatherers wandering the Web following the links they find. If you think you can find music without a title to search for, or the words to a song, try entering a few musical notes and see how far you get. The same goes for pictures. You can input text and have the search engine find a picture related to that text, but you can't input a picture and have a search engine look for a similar or different picture. Not yet anyway. When looking for photographs by Brassai or Ansel Adams, or for the Wright Brothers' first airplane, you execute a text-based query. For the foreseeable future, and for our purposes, content is text, words, sentences, paragraphs, headings, <title>, <h1>, <h2> tags, and META data, and keywords. While this may not be wholly satisfying, it is a workable definition.

Podcasting and Flash Animation

Podcasting is only increasing in importance and will likely live for a long time or give birth to its replacement. Either way, it is well worth discussing. Podcasts are in the same boat as images and all the rest. When you search for a podcast you are conducting a text-based query and will find text information associated with the podcast. This only highlights the importance of the words that you use to title or describe your podcast(s).

Flash animation is the Adobe product used to make those gorgeous effects often seen at the opening of Web sites. We do not recommend relying on Flash, because the files that produce it are not readable by search engines. Flash is fine if it solves a problem, makes a point, or shows users something of value. No argument there, but search engines will not find your Flash because they simply can't read it. That is why we do not recommend opening pages that consist of Flash animation only.

Look at the opening of your Web site. Is it loaded with useless Flash? Flash is useless when it conveys no meaning or contributes no added value to the user. Do you require users to watch the Flash or do you give them a link to end the Flash and enter your site? If you have a link to end the Flash and enter your site, there's a message there. Flash is not content. The designers of the site know that many users will leave rather than wait for the Flash to end. However, Flash animation can be a terrific asset to a site when used properly. For an example of the beauty that Flash can add to a Web site, see *www.sirrebelfilms.com*, created by Mark Coleman. What we are saying is don't use Flash for your entire opening page. As an enhancement, fine. To make the site a thing of beauty, fine. We have no problem with that.

While we are talking about what detracts from a site, let's mention navigational links that are created with javascript. They look great, can be animated, and truly are gorgeous. The problem is that javascript links are not readable by search engines because they don't contain words. For that reason we do not recommend javascript links.

Web pages that are nothing more than a large graphic file are a bad idea because while you may see text on screen there is no search-engine-readable text. As with any graphic file, it is not search-engine-readable because the text is only a picture or graphic of text, not actually words and letters. How can you determine if a site is built this way? At the top of your browser window in your toolbar, you will see the words File, Edit, View, and others. Select and click on View. Look for Source or View Source and click on it. Now you are seeing the nuts and bolts that create what is viewed onscreen. The words you see in the browser should be in the source file.

For these reasons we say that, while sites can and do contain all manner of movies, graphics, directions, maps, buttons, blinking lights, audio, sounds, or songs we, in this book, are only concerned with text because text is what allows search engines to find your site. When you search for a video, a picture, or a song, you are finding the text—the description of it—written in letters and numbers. That needs to be clear.

When You Do Not Want to Be Found by Everyone

This seems like an odd thing to place at the beginning of a book on Web content, but it is a necessary consideration because all Web sites have goals. In the commercial world, you want potential customers to contact you and buy your products, don't you? No, not always. Let's imagine that your client is a pizza restaurant with a large take-out and delivery business. You likely know of restaurants like this. Our pizza shop wants telephone calls and business from people in the geographic area that it serves. Pizza shops have an operating area for their delivery people and for customers who will drive to eat there. Customers from within this area are who our pizza shop wants phone calls from. Calls from outside the operating area take up employee time, contribute nothing, and keep bona fide business from getting through. So you see, it is in the pizza shop's best interest to prominently list what town and state the restaurant is located in and the towns to which it delivers. Including the local telephone number, with area code, at the top of the opening Web page goes a long way to avoid calls from far away. Keep in mind that many town names are duplicated in other states and, when you search for pizza in your town, no search engine will ask you what state you are located in. Search engines are not that smart. Not yet anyway.

Consider a Web site as an employee. It has a job to do. In this case, it is to garner business calls that our pizza shop can fulfill. The Web site's job is to promote calls from within your customer area and eliminate calls from outside that area. So, when we say that the job of Web content is to drive business to you, that's right and wrong. The entire story is this: to drive business to you that you can service and make money from. And to keep you from spending time and money on calls with which you cannot do business. So, if you are a business that caters to local, state, or regional customers, make that clear on your opening page.

Here is an example of unwanted contact. The town of Coventry, Connecticut, used to receive e-mail from people in Coventry, England. This was a time-waster for everyone. It took up the time of the Coventry, Connecticut, town employees and wasted the time of the people in Coventry, England. Online, with e-mail, the people who contact you can be from anywhere in the world. Take steps to ensure that all contact is quality contact, so that this sort of thing does not happen to your clients. Never hesitate to make absolutely clear where you are located and the business area that you serve.

What You Want Content to Do

The goal of your content is identical to the goal of the Web site. No surprise there. For a commercial site the goal is to generate sales. This is done by a phone call, an online store, or, for high-end merchandise, a personal visit to a showroom, dealer, or brick-and-mortar store. To go along with this, the site must support the ease of selling its product. Does the site allow for purchase by credit card? How about PayPal? Can users send you a check? Checks are a bad idea when dealing with the online world, but people still use them. A credit card is far more secure. Also don't forget e-mail and the telephone. Do you have provision for an 800 or 888 number? Even though this is becoming less important with the advent of cell phones, you may want to consider it. The question is how much business comes your way via the phone. With e-mail, you can easily install an automated response e-mailer that sends back an e-mail in seconds. That's fine, but people know that it's automated. E-mail can be a problem if you are not geared up to handle it. It can make you an e-mail slave. Adequate staff is needed to handle timely responses. For that reason we never recommend the use of e-mail unless the client is comfortable with the technology and has the personnel, hardware, and connectivity to handle the traffic. If your client uses the telephone for customer contact now, then simply put their phone number prominently on the top of the opening page. On the contact us page, place the client's snail-mail address and fax number. While we are talking about a fax number, you can suggest that the client use an e-mail/fax service where all faxes arrive in the client's e-mail folder. A fax can be sent from a word processor. This will save your client a fax machine and the telephone line that it requires and will result in a nice reduction in their yearly telephone bill and kudos for you. While there is a monthly fee for the fax service it is less than a dedicated phone line as this is written. This is great for political campaigns where political rivals will send a continuous fax to use up all your paper and all your toner, and maybe destroy your fax machine as well, but that's another story.

Writing for the Client

Writing to be successful means writing content that is targeted to the needs of your client. Before you even begin to write you need to:

» Know the client (or who is paying for it).

» Know what the content is supposed to do. Will it be used on a political Web site or will it be product description? You must know what the content's job is.

» Know how long the content is slated to live. Will it be replaced weekly, daily, monthly, or never? Never is the most likely as people seem to have an aversion to keeping material current. This needs to be kept in mind.

» Meet with the client personally. This is very important to the quality of the content you will be writing. You need to know if the company is 80 or 100 years old, is a good neighbor in its town, and considers itself a family-oriented company that serves the community. Or is the company a brand-new startup: Brash, brilliant, not conservative, stylish, and composed of young people. The style of your writing must reflect that of the client for whom you are writing.

» Avoid allowing the Webmaster getting between you and the client. Tell the Webmaster that you want to be involved in any meetings that will discuss content, the needs of the client, or the purpose of the site. From personal experience, we can tell you that being involved in meetings is very productive. Take your time when in a meeting with the client and listen to the words that people use. You will find the key to building your content. In one meeting, after a couple of hours, we were told that "we are a family-related business." Those words told us who we were dealing with and guided our material. Always make an attempt to meet the client. It's important when you meet the client to be sure that you present an agreeable, non-judgmental business facade because, if the client does not like you, they won't like your writing. Keeping the sympathy of those for whom you write is smart. You are not manipulating anyone. You are keeping the sympathy of the people who pay you, and that is always a smart thing to do.

➡️ Ask specific questions about who the client's customers are because they are the people who will be reading your content. Develop a general customer and give this person a name. Call him Joe or Josephine Customer if you have to. For ease of writing, we will refer to Joe or Josephine simply as Joe and assume that our phantom customer is male.

  ❯ How old is Joe?

  ❯ Where does he live?

  ❯ Does he own a home?

  ❯ Is Joe divorced?

  ❯ Is Joe married?

  ❯ Does Joe have children?

  ❯ How much money does Joe make?

  ❯ What's Joe's educational level? Be prepared for Joe's educational level to run from high school dropout to PhD. This will be the case for any client that deals with people living over a wide geographic area. Our pizza shop is an example, as are fuel oil companies and movie theaters. In this case you write for the lowest education level.

  ❯ Has Joe lived here all of his live? Or did Joe move here from afar?

  ❯ Is Joe a military person?

  ❯ What's important to Joe?

    ◇ Price?

    ◇ Service?

     e of ordering?

     ..me delivery?

⟡ Fuel economy?

⟡ An environmentally friendly product?

⟡ Consistency of product?

⟡ Availability of product?

⟡ Quality of product? While this seems a strange thing to consider, there are items for which we are unconcerned with quality. For example: cheap ballpoint pens, give away products that are made to only look expensive, or gag gifts of little or no value beyond a laugh when given.

Now that you know something about the client and the customer the user is no longer anonymous.

» Look at the design that your Webmaster has roughed out and plan your content accordingly. If you have 30 percent of the onscreen "real estate" taken up with photos, navigation, headings, and a phone number, you need to structure your words accordingly. Don't send the Webmaster 2,000 words, because there is no place to put them all. Do, however, be prepared to cut or add to your words should the design change. And change is a real possibility. Even after the design has been accepted. It has happened to us and will happen to you.

» Do your keyword research. You will need to have keywords before you begin writing because the keywords will need to be included in headings, the body of the text, the META data, and the title tags that you will be writing. If you have not been asked to write title, META, and heading material bring it up to be sure that this is not your responsibility. To be honest, it is in everyone's best interest to have you do this, but that's another story. With the software on the market to optimize a site, you may not be asked to do the research.

All right, now look at the data you've gained. You have met with the client, seen the business, talked with employees, determined what kind of a business they are, how they see themselves, and their customers. You have worked out Joe Customer and know the demographics of the client's customers. You have made friends and shown the client that you are a top flight professional with the ability, brains, skills, and background to do a masterful job with their needs.

So what's next? Start to write, but write for the Web, not for print; and write for the reader, the person who pays for the services or goods, the user. You do not write for the client, the client's sales force, the client's engineers, or for the Webmaster. Only for the user.

On the Web, you write tight. The fewer words you use the better. Less is more in every sense of the word. However, you should use as many words you need to get the message across. We are not saying to dumb down the message. We are saying to write tight; no fluff. You've likely heard that before and I'm sorry to say that you will likely hear it again because it is that important. If you are new to Web writing you have a new skill to master. If you are used to writing or editing theses for PhD students, culture shock is going to come your way. If you have written radio commercials, you're fine. Compared to writing a 15- or 30-second spot for radio, the Web is a breeze. It is all relative to what you are used to. We have included examples that include writing driving directions, how to take something apart and put it back together again, and how to write for those occasions where people could be killed if they don't understand the message.

Fluff Is Not Content

Fluff is not content. Fluff is junk taking up space. It is far better for the client to have a little high-quality content than page after page of fluff. No one is going to read the fluff, even if you think it is serving the purpose of bringing additional users to your site. While some people are more comfortable when their Web site is packed with information, they need to evaluate the quality of the information and just how many users are accessing it. This is easily done by using the diagnostic programs that accompany your Web site or asking your Web master for a report.

12 tips to make your Web site pull its weight

1. Treat your Web site like an employee

Your Web site has a job to do and, as mentioned previously, you should treat it as you would any other employee whose job is sales, marketing, and advertising. To be effective, your Web site needs measurable goals that you can use to determine its effectiveness. To simply throw material on the Web with no clear-cut idea of what the information is supposed to accomplish is a waste of your money and resources. Ask customers how they found your site. Search for your site yourself, in all major search engines. Can you find it?

Review the statistics on the visitors who access your site. How many "hits" per day do you get? How long do they stay? What pages of your site are most popular? This information is invaluable and costs you nothing because your Web statistics contain it.

2. Make your Web site a resource for your customers

This will keep your customers visiting again and again. What to include? Let your customer needs be your guide. Do they need product specifications, current costs, currency conversion, instructions to set up or trouble-shoot complex devices or software? Position yourself as the go-to site for high-quality information, data, and assistance when your customers have problems. This reputation is priceless, and will be reflected in customer loyalty. There is an old saying: "A friend in need, is a friend indeed." When you help someone out of a jam, you make a friend.

3. Tell them what you can do for them

Many people make the mistake of telling the reader what they do, rather than telling the reader what they can do for the reader. There is a critical distinction there, because we all listen to that most important FM station: WIIFM, What's In It For Me. Make clear what you can do for the user. On every major page of your site, list your business name, address, and telephone number, link to your Contact Us page, or include an e-mail link. Every page must be able to stand alone in this regard, because you have no control over what page a user will access when entering your site.

Don't tell people you are a carpenter; tell them that you build homes. Don't say you are a handyman; tell them you will rebuild a bathroom, or a kitchen. Tell people what you can do for them.

4. Include an About Us page and customer testimonials

Here is your chance to tell a prospective customer or client about the company, its senior staff, how long it has been in business, where you are located, and other pertinent material that is important, but does not fit elsewhere on your site. Take care with the style of writing here—not too formal, not too friendly. If you are a high technology firm, a short bio of the senior staff may be called for; if you are an online seller of shoes, that may not be important. Whatever you do, this is the place to tell the world about yourself.

Always include testimonials from your customers, because they show that others have successfully done business with you. Put your testimonials on a separate page and link to it, or put a short testimonial at the top of your main page. Include the name of the person and his or her company or organization. A testimonial like this:

"Great job."

J. Customer, Connecticut

is never as effective as:

"Great service, timely shipping, knowledgeable people."

Janet Customer
Marketing Director
Company Name

The difference is striking. While the first could be from anyone, almost anywhere, the second is from a particular person at an acknowledged company. People aren't stupid; testimonials like the first one border on being bogus. Don't use them.

5. Engage in e-mail marketing

E-mail marketing can be very effective, especially when contacting existing customers.

Ask for an e-mail address when you do business and send notices of sales and special discounts, but be careful that your sales are not periodic, else your customer will simply wait for your next sale. Rather, tie a sale to a one-time event such as a 10-year anniversary sale or other such event that customers won't simply wait for.

If you run a service business and find that contacting your customers is a problem because they are not home when you call, consider using e-mail. It is far more productive than having an employee leave messages on answering machines. Your Web site likely has many e-mail addresses. Use one for each town you work in, or one for each product. This is very cost effective and will simplify your record-keeping and allow you to more easily schedule your services.

6. Publish a newsletter

Give your customers industry news, what's new, products that are coming soon, and what they need to know to use your products better, or for purposes that are not obvious. Str the money-saving aspects and versatility. Keep your newsletter to no more than two pages. Link to more extensive news or events.

Use your e-mail program to make a mailing list that contains the e-mail addresses of all your customers. When you send the newsletter, paste the list into the bcc (blind carbon copy) line and your customers will not see the entire list when they open their mail.

7. Research and determine who your reader will be

Write to that educational or skill level. You may find that your user is very competent and highly experienced in the field. If so, write to an expert level of competence. Should your users be children or teens, use short paragraphs and make your point quickly. This is especially important when writing sales material or when, for example, you need to show the benefits of a new electronic product. Don't hesitate to write one-sentence paragraphs when your users are young people. The rule that says no one-sentence paragraphs was made to be broken.

And this is the prefect situation to break it. Let the needs for clarity dictate how you structure your words. Should you be selling life insurance, answer all questions fully and completely. In this case, your target user wants in-depth information. That is also true when placing highly technical information online for engineers, technicians, mechanics, and others who need to access specific data quickly.

When you need to accommodate users with differing levels of expertise, include a table of contents that shows what is appropriate for a novice and what is for advanced users. A table of contents is invaluable when dealing with complex information, machines, or situations where detail is important. In this way, those in need of specific data can get it quickly. Sites that offer this ability are invaluable and will be remembered, talked about, and linked to. Detail on your Website also makes it more credible.

8. Submit your Web site address to search engines

Submit your Web site's address to Google, Yahoo, AltaVista, and any other search engine, directory, or specialty search engine relevant to your business. To find them search for "search engines" in Google or Yahoo.

For international search engines visit *www.searchenginecolossus.com* to find search engines for 351 countries and territories. This is invaluable if you do business internationally.

When was the last time you tried to find your site in any major search engine? Try it sometime; you may be very surprised at the results you get, or don't get.

9. Make your site easy to navigate

Use consistent navigation links on every major page of your Web site. Be sure that their color, placement, and order are identical from page to page. This is critical to ease of use and user retention, because users like consistency. No user should ever get lost and have no way to return to your main page. People will simply leave your site and go elsewhere. All links must take the user to where they say they will. To intentionally mislabel a link smacks of deception and destroys your credibility. Do not mislead or misrepresent the destination of a link.

10. Install site search capability

Nothing is easier for your customers to use than a site search box. This is used by every major e-commerce site out there. You can use this capability by installing site search capability on your opening page. A search box is a demonstrated asset to any business site, especially when many products, or a great deal of information is presented.

There are many ways to do this. They range from using a major search engine like Google to do the search to installing your own search facility on your Web site. If you use Google, or another external search engine, be aware that the material searched for must have been scanned by Google before it will appear in the search results. So, if you are updating your Web site routinely, this is not a good option because it can be some time before Google re-scans your site. In that case, you are better off with your own search capability because your Web master can simply keep it up to date.

For an excellent search engine you can add to your site see *www.xav.com*, Fluid Dynamics Software Corporation and their Fluid Dynamics Search Engine. We like this product. It does a great job and is easily re-indexed, so important to do after you update the site. This product was recommended to me by Rob Miller at Host Cabin, *www.hostcabin.com*. Rob provides superior customer and technical support.

11. Write for the Web, not for print

Writing for the Web is not like writing for print. People do not read the Web; they scan it looking for pertinent information and specific facts. While people are comfortable reading print in a word-for-word manner, they do not read the Web that way.

Write tight. Use no more words than what are needed. Use no more sentences than required. Users do not want to read fluff, marketing hype, or a sales pitch that you've embedded in valuable information. In fact, users resent it—they resent it a great deal. Don't do it. Make your words all meat and potatoes—solid, easily read and understood, and to the point.

Use simple words; express yourself in simple words that get the message across. Don't dumb down the material. What we are saying is that your intended user must never be forced to look up words to understand what you are writing about. If users can't understand your content they will go elsewhere. We realize that not all content can be understood by everyone. Content must be understood by its intended user for it to accomplish its intended mission. Without a mission, it's fluff. Get rid of it.

12. Advertise your site and business with a media release

Getting the word out that you exist, where you are, and what you sell is critical to your success. Make it a habit to send a media release at least two or three times per year. Sending one quarterly is even better. Always find a tie-in to local, state, or national news and remember that the target of your media release is the media, not your customers. Never expect a thinly disguised advertisement to be picked up as news. It won't.

Writing Your Content

> "Words are like loaded pistols."
>
> —Brice-Parrain

2

Conventional guidelines for good writing hold true for the Web with one major exception. On the Web, you "write tight" using no unnecessary words or sentences. Use commonly accepted language and never simply throw information up and expect users to sort it out and make sense of it. So let's get writing.

The Inverted Pyramid

Those of you who have written newspaper copy will recognize this, as will almost anyone who has published anything. Using an inverted pyramid means placing the most important material first. This technique will provide excellent service for you and your users. First, your client gets the "meat and potatoes" right up front. You do not force the reader to search the text of the material to find the data.

It works well for you because, should the Webmaster or your client need to cut the material, that can be done by removing content from the end of the material. This is why the inverted pyramid style of writing came into being when newspapers were invented. The need to cut material is a daily thing in their world, so the editors developed a method that allowed them to cut whatever was needed from the end of the story.

Write Tight

On the Web, write no unnecessary words, no unnecessary sentences, and no unnecessary paragraphs; prune your words to the essence of what is needed to convey the message. Here are a couple of examples:

Before:

The monthly meeting of the AB Model Aero Club will be held on Friday night, August 31, 2008, at the Anytown Public Library, 1200 Main Street, Anytown, Connecticut. We are located across from the town hall building and next door to the police station. The meeting opens at 7 p.m. with a discussion of old business then moves on to new business before our speaker will talk to us. A speaker will talk about the use of the new glue for balsa wood that we have all been wondering about. There will be a question and answer session and coffee will be brought from the pizza house. We expect the meeting to end at 9pm.

After editing for the Web:

The AB Model Aero Club invites the public to attend its monthly meeting held at 7 p.m. Friday, August 21, 2008, at the Anytown Public Library. A speaker will discuss advances in Balsa wood gluing technology. Questions follow the talk. Coffee will be served.

How to Structure Content

Before you begin writing, think of how you will structure your content and construct a framework that will make it easy for users to find what they're looking for and understand what you are writing. Draw a picture of what your site will contain. This picture is called a site map, and it will contain all the pages that are to be included in the site. Work with the Web master and verify that your plan for the content works within the framework of the design for the site. Knowing something of the overall design is important. We cannot reiterate this enough: Work with the Web master closely and be sure that the design is complete and accepted by the client before you begin to crank out content. Why? When you know the design you know how much "online space" your content must fill. Should the design change, your content may need to be changed as well to fit the new space allocated for your words. Pay close attention to the site design and make it known to the Web master that you want to be involved in redesign meetings or at least notified of design changes in a timely manner. It pays to stay involved.

The site will consist of several to many pages. Each page will be a separate computer file. The content of the About Us page, for example, needs to tell about the business. The Directions page needs to get the user to the business or provide phone and/or e-mail contact options and, perhaps, include a map. The Contact page for a pizza shop will be very different from a software provider. Your product pages will need to explain the goods sold to the buyer, not to the client, to you, or to salespeople. The user is expected to plunk down a bunch of money to buy this stuff. Two books can be a great help with advertising: *Scientific Advertising* by Claude C. Hopkins. We also like *How to Write A Good Advertisement* by Victor O. Schwab.

Words

"Less is more" in a very real sense. No one is impressed by material that contains highfalutin language. In fact, users hate it. Clarity is paramount. Present a clear message in easily understood everyday words. Write clean, concise text that gets the message across in a cogent, understandable, easy-to-read manner.

Never use 10 words when five will do.

Technical and occupational-specific words and phrases are fine when the audience is reasonably expected to have the expertise to understand those terms. Do not use material that only insiders will understand when writing for the general public.

Personalizing the message

When writing personalize the message as much as you can. This is accomplished by using these words:

» You

» Your(s)

» We

Your prose will sing. It is always a pleasure reading the work of an author who took the time to personalize the message. You are writing for people, so write *to* them as well as *for* them. In sales, this is a wonderful way to act like the user has already bought the item. These three words work.

When using *We* you place yourself on a par with the user and so become part of and share the user's experience. This is a powerful technique.

Using "not only" construction

Many excellent writers use *not only* like this: "Not only does our product do this, but it also does that." If you want to tell what something does or does not do why would you start out with a negative? Think about it. Here is a fictional example: "Our fire truck not only puts out wood fires, but oil fires too." We prefer that the message be placed in the positive form of what the fire truck does: "Our fire truck puts out wood fires and oil fires." To begin your message with *not only* just seems strange to us. We realize that is only a way of saying that something does more than one thing or that there is more than one reason or consequence to something, and that's fine. All we object to is starting out with negative construction.

Here are a few more examples:

» Our bicycle not only has 18 speeds, but front wheel drive as well.
Versus: Our bicycle has front wheel drive and 18 speeds.

» Not only is this cleaner, but it is simpler to operate.
Versus: This is cleaner and simpler to operate.

» Not only will you get there in less time, but you will use less fuel.
Versus: You will use less fuel and get there in less time.

Write material that is simple, straightforward, and easy to understand. There is no need to begin your description with *not only*. Describe what something is. Users are smart; they "get it" if you present it. Tell them what things are. Remember that, on the Web, people do not read as they do in print. Plenty of text is searched for, even within a Web page, by using Control-Find, Ctrl-F. Use *not only* construction at your peril and with full knowledge that it can be confusing to a user because users will not be searching for "not only," but words that convey true meaning. Worst of all is the situation in which your user misses the words *not only*. Read over some of the previous examples and ask yourself how they read should the user miss the words *not only*. The decision is up to you. We prefer clear, clean, easy-to-read-and-understand text.

Not just any word will do

Word choice may seem optional or even silly. Nothing could be further from the truth. Word choice matters.

Connotations and how words sound

Consider how a word sounds, before you publish. Things may not sound or read with the meaning you intended. Consider a book published by President Jimmy Carter. He related that, while fishing, a salmon took "a ferocious leap at my fly." He actually had the books still in the warehouse removed and the passage changed to "a ferocious leap at my lure."

Michigan State University advertising professor Vandal Bergh tells us that most top brand names contain at least one of the "positive" sounds, those being: k, p, b, c, d, t, ch, and j.

Positive Words that boost response	
Free	Save
New	Discover
You	Results
Sale	Proven
Introducing	Guaranteed

Negative Words that detract from your message		
Buy	Sell	Death
Failure	Loss	Cost
Bad	Difficult	Order

Emotional words are better than intellectual words

Emotional	Intellectual
Speed	Accelerate
Finished	Completed
Because	For
Bright	Intelligent
Find out	Learn
Answer	Reply
Rich	Wealthy

Use the emotional words. It is far better to speed things up than to accelerate the work; to finish something rather than complete it.

Use present tense rather than past or future

Write in the present. What is going on, happening, or existing in the present is powerful and interesting. It is not history nor is it a future that may never come to pass. It's now, and what is more interesting than that? Don't say you have delighted or made people happy in the past. Tell readers that you will do so in the present. Remember the old saying "What have you done for me lately?" People are much more in tune with present accomplishments than with past performance or future promises. Write in the present. Don't say that the customer will receive a money-back guarantee. Say that the merchandise comes with a money-back guarantee. Don't say the cost is $100 after a money-saving rebate. Tell them that the merchandise comes with a money-saving rebate. Always talk about what the product does and what the buyer receives, not what the product will do or the buyer will receive. Write in the present because, in reality, it is where we always are.

Sentences

Use sentences that are short and to the point and maintain proper grammar. Keep your sentences to no more than 21 words. A sentence length of 15 words is fine. In print, we all use longer sentences. While fine for printed material, avoid long sentences on the Web. Studies relating to how users read online indicate that people prefer shorter sentences. Remember that, on the Web, the size of a user's monitor is not an indicator of the size of the window that the user will have open onscreen. From our own experience, we routinely have windows of all sizes, sometime resizing on the fly multiple times during an online session, and appreciate short sentences. Further, we use Firefox and routinely increase and decrease the font size. This dramatically changes the way Web pages look.

Construction of your sentences is always to be subject first then verb and always in the active form.

YES: John ate an apple.

NO: An apple was eaten by John.

Shakespeare never used one word when 10 would do. That was then; the Web is now. On the Web, Shakespeare's technique would be inappropriate in the context of Web content.

[No disrespect to Mr. Shakespeare intended. He is one of the most successful writers and playwrights in human history, and we have great respect for his skill with the written word and his immense vocabulary. He used more than 29,000 different words in his works. So, we do not criticize him; we admire him. All we are saying is, wordy technique is not appropriate for Web content.]

Do not write fluff. Your writing needs to be boiled down to the essence of what you are saying. What you want are the essentials of the idea or concept. You're in the "no fluff zone" when you write for the Web. Here is a paragraph of text that is loaded with fluff. You won't like the sound if it.

At the present time, we believe that the World Wide Web (henceforth called the Web was created in 1980 by Tim Berners-Lee, who, at the time, was at CERN, The European Organization for Nuclear Research) was designed for scientists, other academics, and technical personnel to collaborate computer to computer in what later became knows as "online." The Web incorporated the use and concept of what was then called electronic mail or e-mail. This, e-mail, was invented, or implemented, in 1971 by Ray Tomlinson, a programmer. As with many great inventions, at first this new way of communicating, which came to be called e-mail, was not thought to be a big deal. In fact, when Tomlinson first showed it to a colleague, he is reported to have said, "Don't show it to anyone! This isn't what we're supposed to be working on."

Okay, that's enough fluff for you to get the idea. It is wordy, and seems to wander with no specific point. We start with the Web and Berners-Lee, then for no reason we are involved with e-mail and its history and creator. The reader has not a clue what we are talking about and why we have made such major digressions. We most love the opening sentence. It is a true testament to fluff. The very fluff of fluff. "At the present time, we believe...." This is about the worst construction we could think of. Please don't write that way unless you need to say you believed something in the past and now believe something else. Simply state what you believe, without using the words *we believe.* Fluff is filler, and filler on the Web is unnecessary and unwanted.

Use common words. When in doubt of the meaning of a word check it on the Merriam-Webster online dictionary, *www.m-w.com.* The Web is no place to show the world how smart you are by using words and phrases not in the common usage of the intended reader. When writing for specific audiences that have a technical or job specific vocabulary go ahead and use appropriate vocabulary. Always write for the user because, when you lose a user, you lose her forever. There are too many other sites out there that may be easier to understand. And let's not forget your client. The client pays your salary, and what you want to give the client are words that gain the trust of the client's customers. So, when you write for the user, you put money in your checking account. Always a good thing.

Paragraphs

Many people only read the first sentence in a paragraph, so make that sentence count. Be sure that the information in the paragraph is accurately summarized in the first sentence. The first sentence, or topic sentence, in a paragraph tells the user what will be found in that paragraph. Material in the topic sentence simply must be found in the paragraph it introduces.

When users are looking for information, they will scan the first sentence of a paragraph.

Keep your paragraphs short, no more than four or five sentences in length. Target your paragraphs to a single thought or concept. Don't have run-ons that cover anything and everything, because users will not wade through all the clutter to find what they want. In fact, users will not read content like you are reading this page, but will scan it looking for specific content. Keep your paragraphs short and use good leading sentences. Your users will be ever so glad you did.

One final note on paragraph length. When writing for children do not hesitate to use one-sentence paragraphs. This violates grammar rules, we know, but it makes the material far easier for young people to read. Do not let rules stop you from writing easy-to-read-and-understand prose.

Headings

Make sure that the all headings introduce the material that they refer to. Users will leave and never return should they find that your site cannot be trusted. Headings can be bolded, of course, to make them stand out and to appear to search engines as important text. The best way to indicate a heading is with HTML heading tags. These tags range from <H1>, the largest, to <H6>, the smallest. Search engines use heading tags to assign importance to the text they contain. So, use them judiciously, placing the most important material within <H1> tags and less-important material in <H2> tags. At this time Google uses only <H1> and <H2> tags. By the time you read this, that may have changed.

Calling attention to text

You will always be running across text that you want to call attention to. For that you can simply display the text in bold with the bold tag, <B>. Do not use bold text indiscriminately or overuse it. Only bold text that is important, but less important that what is contained in <H1> or <H2> tags.

Also, it is a good idea to stay away from underlining as a way of calling attention to the importance of text. Remember: On the Web, links are underlined. When you underline text, users will think it is a link and may try to follow a link that is not there. This is confusing and frustrating. Italics do not render well onscreen, in our opinion, and we do not recommend that you use italics to indicate the importance of text. As you have no control over the resolution, size, or quality of the user's screen, it is best not to use italics at all.

Some writers place important material in uppercase, LIKE THIS. Avoid using all capital letters. It is a poor technique, is difficult to read, means nothing to search engines, and just plain looks lousy. Also, many users will read uppercase as shouting. In fact, in chat rooms, on blogs, and other places online shouting is precisely what uppercase indicates. Avoid this technique. Users don't like it and neither do we. If you have to resort to shouting your opinion at users, you are in the wrong line of work. As every schoolchild knows, when people resort to shouting it indicates either a weak position or an inability to articulate ideas in a cogent, intelligent manner. You are a writer and far too intelligent to resort to this, so don't.

Links

Be sure that links take the user to where the link's title says it does. It is frustrating to follow links and find that they do not go to their titled location. Links that take the user to unintended destinations are a disaster. Never have a link take the user to an "Under Construction" page. Rather than insult people, simply do not put the link and the page it refers to online until the material is ready. Be sure that all links are working by checking them. All it takes is one mistyped letter to break a link. When a link is correctly spelled and remains non-working check the spelling of the file the link goes to. If the file name is wrong, simply change the spelling of the link to reflect the file name. Verify that every link on the site is updated to reflect the actual spelling of the file name.

When linking to a file that the user may want to download use this format:

File name, file type, size in bytes.

Like this: Antique cars [PDF 5MB].

This way the user can gauge the download time. Many people use dial-up connections and have much longer download times than cable or broadband connectivity. Another good thing is to indicate when a link will take the user to another Web site. Show the link something like this: More about fuel cells at CNN. This tells the user what the link concerns and that the destination is CNN. Also, talk to your Web master about having the link open in a new window. This way, if the user closes the window containing the story on fuel cells at CNN, the original Web site will still remain on his or her desktop. This is the preferred way to do this because the user can easily return to your client's Web site. Always make things easy for users.

Links are the big gun in the Web's arsenal, of that there is no doubt. This does not mean you should use them everywhere for everything. If you can adequately present the information without using a link, do so. Make your link description crystal clear. If you want to add additional material do this <a href=http://www.webaddress.com title='This information will pop up when the mouse is placed on the link.'>Link description</a>. For more information on formatting a link's title see Links and formatting of title information in Appendix C.

For cross-references or ancillary information that may be nice to know, but not critical, use link titles like this: "See also..." or "For more on widgets..." or "Background information on widgets." This does your users a real service because those who want more explanation can get more, and others can avoid following a link that offers them little. On the Web people want specific information, only reading background when it helps them understand the primary data that they are after.

Ambiguous link titles

Users want clear, unambiguous link titles. When you name a link "Next" users do not know whether that means the next page or next chapter. This is confusing. Write the link text in straightforward, easy-to-understand language that tells users precisely where the link will take them.

Always seek to use keywords in link titles. This is noticed by search engines and will help raise the sites search engine status. Also, it will bring people to the site when they search for those keywords.

Captions

Captions identify graphics, photos, and other non-text information. Always caption your material, but do not use words that appear in headings on the page where the caption is located or you will confuse search engines. You do not want people finding the caption when they are looking for information. If your graphic's meaning is obvious leave the caption out, as there is no point in adding redundant material, unless you need to refer to a specific graphic. Avoid labeling graphics as Figure 1 or Figure 2. That sort of nomenclature is not descriptive. Also this is not needed if the graphics are so completely different that no one could possibly confuse them.

Whitespace

Don't crowd information together. Whitespace is not wasted space, but a bona fide design element, and a good one. Knowledgeable use of whitespace can make your Web site sing, enhance its readability, and just plain look great.

Bullets or unnumbered lists

Set out your information in bulleted lists. Bullets are especially useful when the information you present does not need to be in a specific order. What's a bullet?

- This is a bullet.
< This is as well.
· Here is another bullet.

You get the idea. On the Web, almost any graphic can be used as a bullet. Ask your Web master about this. Please don't make the site garish by using blinking or flashing bullets. You will just make users crazy. Good taste is paramount when you select your graphics.

Numbered lists

Use a numbered list when the order of entries is important. When using a numbered list, be sure that the material is in the proper order. The Web browser will number the list from number one to the greatest number required. Should you need to rearrange the content of the list, the numbers will always run from lowest to highest. Your numbered list can be composed of: numbers, uppercase letters, lowercase letters, uppercase Roman Numerals, or lowercase Roman Numerals. You can also begin numeration at a specific value other than one. Like this:

<ol> begins a numbered list.

<ol start=5> begins numbering with the number 5.

<ol type=A> begins numeration with uppercase A. The next item in the list will be uppercase B.

<ol type=a> begins numeration with lowercase a. The next item in the list will be lowercase b.

<ol type=I> begins with uppercase Roman Numerals.

<ol type=i> begins with lowercase Roman Numerals

<ol type=I start="7"> begins numeration with uppercase Roman Numerals at number 7, VII.

Note on quotation marks: If you have problems transposing your word processor's quotation marks, open the file in an ASCII editor like EditPlus or Notepad, and substitute ASCII quotation marks. This should not be a problem if you export your file to HTML, but may be if you cut and paste from a word processor directly into an HTML file. Forewarned is forearmed as dear old Mom used to say. We bring this up because small problems like this can cause you major headaches until they are routed out. Limit your online list to nine items or less and to no more than two levels. For instance:

<ol type =A>

<li>First item

<ol type=1><li> Additional information under First item</ol>

<li> Second item

</ol> end list

In your browser this will look like:

   A. First item

      1. Additional information under First item

   B. Second item

Units of measure

Always include the units of what you are referring to. If you are referring to miles, feet, pounds, centimeters, meters, or kilometers, say so. In mathematical equations, list all units and show every item in your calculations. This is true for salesmen as well as engineers. When you put material on the Web that users will use to determine how much of something they need to purchase, leave nothing out.

If your online program determines how many square yards of carpet, for example, are needed to cover a floor, clearly show that the user is to enter the room dimensions in feet and that the calculator determines, and returns, the amount of carpet required in square yards, if that is the case. When writing an equation, clearly include all units and the unit associated with the solution of the equation. Do not simply return a bare number. For example, it is 110 miles from Hartford to our location. It is not 110 from Hartford to our location. The units mean everything; do not neglect them.

Metric and American units

When you wish to include both American and metric units place the metric units in parenthesis. Like this:

❥ 100 statute miles (160 kilometers)

❥ 1 inch (2.54 cm)

Uppercase M refers to mega, or one million. Do not use it to refer to micro (one-millionth). For micro use mu (μ). For example, use 150 μm to refer to 150 millionths of a meter. Lowercase m refers to milli or one-thousandth and M refers to million. Do not confuse them. There is a large difference in one million of something and one-thousandth of something. Exercise caution when using M in conjunction with tons, as in MTON because it can refer to metric ton or megatons. Make it obvious what you are referring to. Define the term if you have to or include a key.

How to write and present numbers

When dealing with numbers from zero to ten, write them out. For numbers greater than ten, use the numbers themselves: one, five, ten, 11, 12, 1,000.

❥ One million or 1 million. Using the numeral is very effective with large numbers when precision is not required and is easily read on the Web.

Use commas in large numbers:

❥ 37,165

Use a leading zero in decimals:

❥ Yes: 0.375

❥ No: .375

Show numbers as numerals online

Online it is best to use numbers as numerals despite what you will read in the style guides. It is far easier for a user who is scanning your site to read, interpret and understand 23 rather than twenty-three. It has been found in eye-tracking studies by Jakob Nielsen, *www.useit.com/alertbox/writing-numbers.html*, "...that numerals often stop the wandering eye and attract fixations...." So, what is more easily read online is what you want. For example:

❥ Two trillion rather than 2,000,000,000 or 2x10⁹.

❥ Compromise? Sure. Write 2 trillion rather than 2,000,000,000,000.

Then there is the international audience where you need to tell them what you are referring to:

- One trillion or 1,000 billion. Why? A billion in the United States is not a billion in Europe. They refer to different quantities.

- When using an abbreviation, like 1TB, to indicate one-terabyte, you had best explain it and other unusual or very large abbreviations as well. Explain that 1TB is 1,000 GB or 1,000,000 megabytes. These explanations inform the user precisely what one terabyte is in terms that are relevant to the user. Also, some units can actually vary from one country to another. By defining what the terms mean, you can alleviate a great deal of confusion.

When you need to refer to indefinite numbers, do so this way: Thousands of people attended the rally. Never write: 1,000s of people attended. In this context, the term *thousands* is not data; it is not an exact or precise measure, but only intended to indicate the magnitude of the number you are talking about.

- The book had hundreds of pages.

- We were held up for hours.

When using numbers to compliment or to complain, precision is far better. When complaining: We were held up for six hours and 15 minutes, or simply, for over six hours.

When using bullets, do not hesitate to open with a number. While this is a no-no in print it is very acceptable online because it is easier for the user to read.

- 3 million were sold.

Digits are easier to read and lend an air of accuracy to your data as well. This goes against what you have been told for print material. Like the man said, "Rules are made to be broken." What the man did not say, but what is also true, is, "Rules are made to be broken, after you know them and have a bona fide reason to break them."

Time of day

It is often necessary to include the time of day in your writing. To do so in an unambiguous manner is always what you want. Terms such as *noon* and *midnight* avoid confusion. Especially when you think about the confusion that 12 p.m. or 12 a.m. can create. It is much easier to simply state 12 noon. By using 24-hour time you remove all doubt. When writing, 13:00 hours, you refer to 1 p.m., 12:00 is noon and of that there is no doubt. Ditto for 24:00.

Writing 9 a.m. until noon or 2 p.m. to 5 p.m. leaves no doubt as to what time you are referring to. If you want to include 24-hour time, feel free to do so: 2 p.m. (14:00). Do not use 24-hour time alone unless you are sure that your users understand it. Many people do not understand 24-hour time, so never use it alone for the general population. Should you need to refer to time zones do not hesitate to add them. This is especially important for travel sites or where you are dealing with international users. Writing 9 a.m. EST leaves no doubt. This can be particularly important if you are located in the vicinity of two time zones or are conveying arrival or departure time.

Day, date, and year

The Web is cluttered with a vast amount of out of date material. Do a search for an event and you can easily turn up material that is years, even decades, out of date. Do everyone a favor and include the year in your dates. It is troubling to read about an event only to find out that what you are reading is years old. Sometimes data on a Web site is not updated or removed—ever. Write like this, or some other reasonable format:

Wednesday, October 26, 2007—2 p.m. until 5 p.m.

or

The event runs from October 1, 2007, to October 7, 2007.

This way the reader can easily determine if the information is for the current event or last year's. If at all possible, make it a point to remove out-of-date material. People want to know when the next meeting will be held. Keep your information fresh and up to date. Users will be glad you do.

Acronyms

Acronyms are shortened references to words or phrases. When you use one, define the first appearance of it—always.

- Emergency Medical Technician (EMT)
- Digital Volt Meter, DVM
- VAC (Volts Alternating Current)
- VDC, Volts Direct Current
- mAh (milliamp hour)

There are some notable exceptions to this rule:

❯ NASA, FBI, IRS, USA

Avoid using mailing abbreviations (for example, CT versus Connecticut). The abbreviation CT is for mailing addresses. Should you need to indicate the name of a state, spell it out completely.

As you have no control over how a user enters a Web page, you have no control over what, if anything, was read before the user got there. So, when you use an acronym define it. Do not assume that the user has read previous material on other pages.

Use the active voice

In our society, we like information presented so that we know the subject first, then the action, and then the result of that action. In the active voice it is the subject who performs the action. When you write, phrase your message in the active voice, never in the passive voice.

Say: *Willie drove the car into a tree.*

Not: *A car was driven into a tree by Willie.*

As Willie is the subject of the sentence, he is placed first in the sentence construction. Next comes the verb—the action—and lastly the result of that action.

Say: *Nuclear power generates 19 percent of the electricity used in the United States.*

Not: *Nineteen percent of the electricity used in the United States is generated by nuclear power.* (While this is not wrong, it does keep vital information to the last words. That is what you do not want to do.)

State your position strongly, in the active voice. Your job is to inform, educate, motivate. It is not your job to force users to figure out what point you are making. A friend of ours once wrote: "It seems that the result of using this device in enhanced access to data." This memo was to be sent to a vice president. He asked our opinion. After editing: "This device offers us the ability to collect and analyze high quality data in real time." Say what you mean. Do not force the reader to figure out what you are saying. The reader does not know what you mean. Write in clear unambiguous language that is appropriate to the reader's needs and the decision that the reader is expected to make from the material. In this case a vice president was depending on an analysis of the device. And he got an excellent analysis. What was lacking was the message that the analysis produced, not the work that produced it. Do you see that wishy-washy writing could cause a complete and utter disaster because it did not convey the result of the work behind it? Always write what you mean in an active unambiguous voice. Always.

Look at it this way

When people are in trouble, they call, "Help!" They do not say, "At this location we require assistance." Put the message, what matters, first. Tell the reader right up front what you are talking about, what it is that what you are talking about is doing, and the result of what you are talking about as done. Isn't that a mess? Yes, of course it is. Would it not be clearer if we had written, tell the reader what you are doing and the result of the action. Isn't that better? Or you could perhaps, maybe, kind of, well you know, say, "Better it is." But then you would sound like Yoda. Not a good thing. Write for clarity and understanding. A good thing that is.

Exceptions to the rule

Are there exceptions to this? Yes, sure there are, especially on the Web where readers scan text looking for keywords. In fact, studies (see: *useit.com*) show that users read in an F shaped pattern, often reading the first two words of a paragraph. Knowing this, it is in everyone's best interest to place the most important words and keywords first. Are we saying to break the rules? Yes, absolutely we are. Your first responsibility is to be sure that the reader can make sense out of and find your content. The rules of grammar exist to make the language readable. Literally, to structure the words into meaningful ideas and concepts. It is the meaningful ideas that the rules are designed to protect and to that end you must bend your efforts. Never let a rule stand between you and the clarity, ease of understanding; or ability of the user to find material. Do whatever it takes to publish quality content. That effort includes making material easy to find. It's a fact that we need to get the first two or three words right because that is all that many users will see when they scan a Web page. So, for the elements that stand out on a page, headings, subheads, summaries, captions, links, and of course bulleted or numbered lists do not hesitate to place what is most important first even if you create content in the passive form. It is better that passive form content be found rather than active voice content be missed.

We are talking about passive headings, not the text of the document. For body text, avoid the passive form, but not in the headings. First get your material found. Then get your material read.

Lending Credibility to Your Writing

People are bombarded with messages on television, on the radio, from spam, e-mail, and pop-up advertisements on the Web, in newspapers, in the car, on their cell phone, on signs on the side of the road, from everywhere. Literally, from everywhere. In fact, soon you will find advertisements on gasoline pumps. Yes, there are Internet-capable gas pumps to show you ads while you fill up. You will hear advertising people say that they have got to cut through the clutter, meaning that they must craft an ad that people will read, pay attention to, and act on. We writers have similar responsibilities when we create Web content. There are things you can do to lend credibility to the message.

You can have your words backed up by the testimonial of an expert in the field. If you do this the expert must have what it takes to back up the statement in no uncertain terms. To have the man on the street say that something is good means nothing. Choose your experts with care. Then there is always the endorsement from a well-known or famous person. Many people in entertainment and sports do this sort of thing. That person could be an athlete, musician, or movie star. The fact that someone with name and face recognition is plugging your product will get a lot of people to stop and see what he or she has to say. And, if that is what you are after, it may be enough. For many products it is. Where this breaks down is in medical and other needs of a personal nature. Here you want people who have successfully undergone the procedure and are willing to let their story be told with their name attached. This is very powerful and not to be underestimated. We suggest that a short background sketch be included. Just enough for the user to realize that this person is your normal man or woman on the street. Just like your user is. With the ability to use downloads and audio/video technology, you can easily write up a script and place a video on your client's Web site. With a little extra effort you can even include a podcast.

Details

It is said that "the devil is in the details." That is certainly true. However, for us, it is not the devil, but credibility that is in the details. The more detail you include in the description, the more credibility the user will give you.

This shows people that you know what you are talking about. Nothing pegs you as an expert better than knowing your subject's details, and people with expert knowledge certainly know them. While users are free to agree or disagree with this or that no user will ever say that you don't know what you are talking about when you have showed that you demonstrate expert knowledge. When you choose someone to quote or to use for a testimonial as an acknowledged expert, be absolutely sure that who you quote truly is an expert. You don't get a second chance to get this right.

When you listen to someone describe what it is like to sky dive, ski, or win a race it is their details that convey the meaning: how hard the climb, how cold the nights on the mountain, the smell of the camp stove, how bad or surprisingly good the rations were. These and a thousand other details separate the person who actually climbed the mountain from someone who just wants you to think that he or she climbed the mountain. Use details to make your words sing with authenticity. Where do the details come from? Research. Do your homework.

Make meaningful associations

There is no finer tool in writing than the use of comparison. When you use this technique be sure to choose things to compare that are meaningful to your readers. This applies especially to statistics. To say that more people are killed by falling coconuts than people die in shark attacks is fine, but just how many people are killed by sharks and what has that got to do with coconuts? Are you saying tropical islands are dangerous places in and out of the water? Or saying that a cannon-ball-sized coconut dropped from 50 feet can kill you? *Gee, there's a surprise.* Or are you trying to compare the probability of shark attack to that of getting hit by a falling coconut? Well, if you spend any time in the tropics you soon learn to stay out from under coconut trees. So, to what does this relate? That is the question that you do not want the reader asking. You want your statistics to be meaningful, and by themselves statistics rarely are.

Statistics

Use statistics that mean something and be careful when you use them. We recently received some sales hype and were told that every year 50 percent of this outfit's customers stayed with the company. Well then, 50 percent leave every year, which seems like some serious turnover. The statistic meant one thing to the salesman and something totally different to us. Statistics matter. They affect your credibility as do the words you use and your ability to write well.

Earlier we talked about coconuts and shark attacks. Consider:

» For the years 1959–2006 the total deaths by lightning in the United States was 1,916. Deaths from shark attack were 23. Lightning is a threat everyone on earth faces and it is far more credible than comparing to death by coconut.

» In the years 1990–2006 there were 16 fatalities from collapsing sand holes and 12 from shark attacks. This, at least, gives numbers that are relatively close in magnitude.

» Bicycles. For the years 1990–2006 there were 12,974 deaths from bicycle accidents. In the same time period there were 12 shark attack fatalities in the United States. Bicycles are clearly a far greater threat than sharks. Aren't they?

Now we get to the actual threat posed versus the perceived threat posed. For this there is no better example than smoking and the threat it poses to the smoker and others around him.

Consider these death rate extrapolations for smokers in the United States: 440,000 die per year; 36,666 die per month; 8,461 die per week; 1,205 die per day; 50 die per hour. These numbers are grim, as they were no doubt intended to be. We offer them here to show you that words matter. How you structure content matters. Numbers matter. Sometimes those numbers are people who you or your user may have known and loved. These numbers are so large that they rival battlefield conditions. In World War II, the United States suffered 416,800 military deaths. Smoking kills more than that every year. Do you see the power of choosing the right statistic? When meaningful to the reader, statistics can be powerful devices that can alter behavior, if you can get the user to pay attention and take them to heart.

Here is something in a lighter tone. Do you remember the Wendy's advertisement "Where's the Beef?" It was masterfully done and resulted in a 31 percent increase in sales and elevated the 80-year-old Clara Pellar to the status of a semi-celebrity. This was a successful campaign because on TV the viewer could see what was being talked about. This is the "see for yourself" approach of influencing people. Should you decide to use this approach you must be very careful. You need to be sure that the user sees what you see. Remember the salesman and his 50-percent retention rate statistic? It told two stories. "See for yourself" is a powerful technique when used properly. Be sure that what you ask people to see is what they do see. Do this by testing your content. Also, whenever you ask users to make a decision, you must be absolutely sure that the decision that they actually make is the one you want them to make.

Predictions

People are not noted for their capability to predict. Don't ask users to make predictions based on the data or argument you present. Think of our favorite salesman again, the one who talks about a 50 percent retention rate. Do not ask users to make assumptions or draw conclusions from presented data. You must make the conclusions for them and tell them what that those conclusions are. Tell them in plain, easy-to-understand language. Never lose control of your content.

Things to avoid

There are many things that can hurt your prose. Here are a few to be avoided at all costs. What is written for a Web site can be a thing of beauty and success, or hammer the site and the business that owns it beyond belief. The following is not a complete list of what not to do. It is a list of things that we've run into over the years in print, on the Web, and in dealing with highly intelligent people. This is not an intelligence thing because it is not the lack of intelligence that creates problems. It is the assumption that there is nothing wrong with doing things the way they have been done, and an inability to see the site as the user sees it. The only way to effectively combat this is to have the material proofread and looked at by a wide range of people and then acting on the feedback.

Do not use uncommon acronyms

Abbreviations made up on the fly are a mistake. Don't use them.

❯ Do not abbreviate police officer as p.o. This is not common. Yes, we've seen it done in print.

❯ Never use a commonly accepted abbreviation to refer to something else. For example EMT is universally accepted as referring to emergency medical technician. We have seen it used to refer to emergency monitoring technician.

❯ Small, or lowercase, m refers to milli, or one-thousandth. Uppercase M refers to mega, or one million.

Cute or non-standard spelling

While it may be very cool to write things like the number 4 rather than using the word *four* or *for*, lowercase i rather than uppercase I, and made-up abbreviations that are fine for a small segment of the population, such as the drivel that is used in text messaging, create a disaster online.

Do not write this way. When used in content it is absolutely without redeeming value. When used in a Web address it's deadly. When people look for a Web site they will spell things correctly. Should a Web address not be spelled right it will never be found. Just think of all that work and effort wasted. Spell words correctly. If the Web address you want is taken, find another one that you can spell correctly. Never intentionally spell words wrong. Many people will be reading your words. Write for everyone. If you don't, you will alienate all the people who can't figure out what you are saying and that is the Kiss of Death to your client, your reputation, your future, and your checkbook.

Insulting, vulgar, obscene, hate-filled, or derogatory language

This only turns people off. They will leave your site, your client, and you forever. To gain widespread support, readership, and an airing of your views your content must be read. Always write for the reader in a manner that the reader does not find offensive, because if no one reads your words no one gets exposed to your ideas. And ideas are important. You are an intelligent, articulate person or you would not be creating Web content. There is no need or excuse for you to be vulgar and insulting. It only makes you and your content look bad.

Under construction

Never put a page on the Web with this as its content. Wait until the content is complete and then put the page up. No one wants to see Under Construction when they follow a link that is supposed to contain information.

Welcome to...

Do not welcome users to a site. We do not say this to be rude. It's simply offers the user no value and takes up precious on-screen real estate. Professional Web developers know better. Also never place "Welcome to..." in the site's <TITLE> tag. To do so is deadly. Search engines will never find the site. Think about it: How many people will search for "Welcome to..."? None, because those words have nothing to do with the business. Many Web sites make this mistake. Try going to any search engine and searching "Welcome" you will get hundreds of thousands of hits. To find one particular site is impossible.

Humor

Use it with caution. What is funny to you may not be to your users. Also, what is funny locally may not play well in another part of the country or to international users. Puns are especially dangerous to use if you expect international users to visit your site. Here is an example: We published a short piece with a newsletter based in London England and used the word *pants*. The editor changed it to trousers because in England "pants" refers to underwear. When dealing with international users it is imperative that your content be proofread by a knowledgeable person who knows the culture(s) that will be reading it. Take nothing for granted.

Jargon

Do not use jargon. It is job-specific and may or may not be in use industry wide. Further, people just starting out in the business may not recognize it or know what it means. All industries have jargon. If you need or wish to use it, then define it. There are many ways to do this, including making what looks like a hypertext link that pops up a definition of the word. Or better yet, make a definitions section on the page. This is actually done in procedures and other industrial and occupational documents. By placing the definitions section at the front of the document, the user sees it before the body of the material is read. So, if you use jargon, define it. Should you find more than one definition for a term, be very careful. Some documents are so important that, if misunderstood, someone could be killed or seriously injured. When this happens, stop the job and get the information straightened out by a subject matter expert, SME, who knows the industry.

Names and positions

You will need to refer to people, titles, and the positions that they hold in a company or organization. Keep in mind:

> ➋ People come and go from positions. Should a user inadvertently ask for someone by name, the user may be told that the person is no longer with the company. This creates confusion and needless problems when the user only wants to speak to the position, not necessarily the person in that position.

- When people leave the company or are promoted, the Web site must be edited to reflect that. Until the edit is completed the Web site will be out of date.

- Some sites list the names of senior management and their e-mail addresses, and some do not. This can be a sensitive issue. Find out what the customer wants before you chase around for hours getting names and e-mail addresses only to find that the client does not want that information on the Web.

- When publishing telephone, cellular telephone, or fax numbers triple-check them and have them verified for accuracy.

Sometimes it is best to list people's title and not their name. Here is an example: If you are interested in joining our club, contact the Membership Committee or attend a meeting. Also, there are times when you need only state: Contact customer service at.... Or, see our FAQ. These comments provide the necessary information and mention no specific name(s).

There are times when then the names of top executives and others will need be placed on the Web. There are good and valid reasons to do this, including showing the world that your company has expertise and experience on board. When using the names, and sometimes pictures, review the information that is included. Be sure to tell the people who have their names online to expect to receive resumes, letters, and sales material in their published mailbox. Consider using the unspammable e-mail code in Appendix H. This will go a long way to keep the e-mail addresses you list from being read by a robot and added to spam lists. The people who have their e-mail addresses listed will appreciate that. Also, you might suggest that any publically published e-mail addresses go to a special mailbox and not be used as a main e-mail address. Also, this e-mail address needs to be checked regularly because there could be an e-mail there that leads to more business.

Technical content

You may be called upon to write for scientists or engineers, or simply to make a technical report Web-ready. While you can simply save the material in HTML format from within your word processor, we don't recommend depending on that because sometimes things just don't get rendered correctly. This is one time where a technical background will serve you well. If you are a technical person with a mathematics or engineering background this sort of thing will pose little problem. Should you not have technical background what follows may be of help. In mathematics, science, engineering, and chemistry, equations are everyday stuff. They are literally the language of science.

You are not going to have to do the mathematics or the science, but you will need to be able to put the equations and report into Web-ready format. Luckily this is not terribly difficult. You will make extensive use of your ^{superscript} and $_{subscript}$ functions.

Superscript and subscript

Your word processor (we specifically refer to WordPerfect, Microsoft Word, and other advanced products) has the ability to place text into superscript or subscript. This can also be done in HTML with the <sup> and <sub> tabs. The entire tag looks like this: ² and ₂. The second tag, the one with the slash [/], ends the superscript or subscript and returns the browser to its previous text setting. So when using HTML to make x^2 your tag will look like this: x². In a word processor it will simply look like this: x^2.

Chemical symbols

Chemicals are represented in terms of their molecular makeup. For example, water is commonly referred to as H_2O, meaning two hydrogen atoms and one oxygen atom have gotten together to create water. By using nothing more complex that the subscript and superscript you can write any molecular formula. What you will not be able to do is draw a picture of the molecule. For that you will need a graphics engine. We recommend you let the client do that. Have them make the graphic and send it to you for inclusion into your text. Be sure to coordinate this with the Web master so that the graphic and its caption are properly placed on the page. If the caption and text are highly technical, have it verified by your subject matter expert, SME, for accuracy. The people who will be seeing this will be technically savvy, and this needs to be absolutely correct.

Mathematics

You may at some time work for professionals who will need to place technical, mathematical, or other such material on the Web. When that day comes, what follows may just get you the job. Don't turn down the gig because you don't have a great technical background. It is your writing skills that are needed. They'll do the math.

The table below contains some mathematics symbols that you will be likely see in the client's data. Some of these symbols are easily created, like arrows or the plus (+) and minus (-) signs. Others you will find are beyond HTML's ability to create. What to do? Use your word processor's equation editor and export the material to HTML. Once you have the material in HTML format you simply incorporate the file into your material. Note: Do not expect to be able to edit your equations once they are in HTML format. When an edit is needed you will most likely need to use your equation editor and do another export to HTML. So be sure what you export is finished and ready for final use.

Some Mathematical Symbols			
$\geq$	Greater than or equal to	$\rightarrow$	Arrow right
$\leq$	Less than or equal to	$\leftarrow$	Arrow left
$\approx$	Approximately equal to	$\uparrow$	Arrow up
$\pm$	Plus or minus	$\downarrow$	Arrow down
$\times$	Multiply	$\int$	Integral
$\div$	Divide	$\sqrt{}$	Square root
$+$	Add	$\sqrt[n]{}$	Nth root
$-$	Subtract or minus		Long division
Σ	Summation	$\therefore$	Therefore
$\ni$	Such that	$N^{Superscript}_{Subscript}$	Superscript and Subscript

On the keyboard you will find:
- = Equal to symbol
- + Plus or addition symbol
- - Minus or negative symbol
- x Multiplication
- / Division, written 10/5 to indicate that 10 is divided by 5. Using parenthesis and spaces makes this easier to read and understand: (10/5) = 2.
- % Percent symbol
- $ Dollar symbol for United States currency
- ( ) Open and close parenthesis
- [ ] Open and close brackets
- { } Open and close braces

It is interesting to note that the cents symbol for United States currency may not be found on your keyboard. When listing prices this can be a problem as you can't easily show how many cents something costs, so for a 50-cent item write $ 0.50. Be sure to include the leading zero and the dollar sign so that the user does not mistake the price for 50 dollars. The actual symbol for cents, ¢, can be likely be found in your word processor's typographic symbols listing.

Engineering notation

This notation expresses things like this:

2.00 $(10)^3$ meters is two kilometers. Engineers like their exponents in multiples of three. Like this: $(10)^3$, $(10)^6$, $(10)^9$, $(10)^{12}$, $(10)^{-3}$, $(10)^{-6}$.

In the example above, 2.00 $(10)^3$ meters, the exponent 3 means that you have a one followed by three zeros—1000—or one thousand. 2.00 multiplied by 1,000 is 2,000.

Scientific notation

Scientists often use very large or very small numbers, requiring the use of exponents. For example when they write the speed of light in space they do so like this: 2.998 $(10)^{10}$ centimeters per second. So, where an engineer would have the exponent, in this case the ^{10}, an engineer would prefer to see something divisible by 3. An engineer would write it: 29.97 $(10)^9$ centimeters per second.

You won't be responsible for the mathematics, but you will be responsible for being able to write out the equations. Now you can, with little more than using superscript and subscript.

Some Examples

The following are some examples of content. They include material on writing instructions for a lawn mower, a non-working computer, writing directions, making assumptions, and writing directions.

Instructions

Instructions need to be presented in a coherent, logical format and in the sequence that the activity is to be accomplished. When you are writing instructions to sharpen the blade on a rotary lawnmower, you first need to ensure user safety so that the user does not inadvertently kill or seriously injure him or herself when following your directions. This information is vital and needs to appear first.

Always tell the user what to do. Never tell the user what not to do. Let us digress for just a minute to giving directions to someone who is to drive from one place to another. When giving driving instructions you always tell the driver where to turn, what to look for. Have you ever had someone tell you, "don't go left" when they mean "go right"? Never tell people **what not to do** because sometimes they misread or do not hear the word *not.* (To say or write *don't* is far worse because the apostrophe t (don't) can be missed when read or not heard when spoken. The consequences of this can be disastrous.)

When people could be killed

Consider: Don't Enter When Red Light Flashing

Versus: Your Death or Serious Injury Will Result From Entrance
            When Red Light Is Flashing—This Door Is Locked. Obtain
            Key at Control Room.

Which is more powerful? Would you walk past a flashing red light? But what if the light is not working or burned out? That eventuality is planned for. The area is locked and the key is only available at a single location.

The word *Your* is added to the sign to personalize the message. It is you who may die or be seriously injured. It gets your attention, and may save a life or lives because many people cut corners and do things they should not do. That is why the door is locked. This is not fiction. Industrial facilities routinely lock people out of dangerous places. Where people lives are at risk, do not beat around the bush; tell them so in clear language.

This is the ultimate example of writing for the reader. Here is 'What's In It For Me,' WIIFM, in action. What's In It For Me? You get to live. You may think that what you write on the Web may not be that dire. That may not be the case if you are writing maintenance or equipment replacement instructions for industrial facilities. That may not be the case at all.

In general, instructions need to convey:

» What the job is or what will be accomplished when the job has been completed.

» The tools required, including test and measurement devices, paperwork or permission to enter the work area, current data on air quality, radiation levels, and other pertinent area conditions that can affect worker health and safety.

- The replacement parts required, including cleaners, solvents, materials to absorb water or oil—that sort of thing.

- The relative difficulty for a homeowner or other novice. This can be omitted for professionals.

- The approximate length of time it will take to accomplish the job, how many people are needed, and ancillary services like security, a crane, a truck, or equipment that will be supplied by others. This is important for professionals as well as novices.

- Safety information and instructions on how to take equipment safely out of service and tag it as such, if appropriate. Tagging is beyond the scope of this book. In any facility that uses colored tags it is of paramount importance to get them absolutely correct. People can be killed if the tagging is not correct, and we do not exaggerate for effect.

- Also, if needed, include information on how to test equipment to verify that it is safely out of service or no longer connected to electric power, steam, water, or other hazard. Any equipment that needs to be taken out of service must be specifically listed as to what it is and where it is. Also, the procedure to do that must be referred to by name, number, or title. Never simply tell someone to go somewhere and turn something off. Things must be done right or not at all. The impact of doing things in an uncoordinated manner can be dire, dangerous, and expensive. Safety is of paramount importance. Never cut corners in your writing. Never, ever say to yourself, "They know that," and leave something out.

- List each step logically and tell the reader of any parts that are to be retained for reassembly or reuse.

- Should reassembly include fine adjustments, specific tolerances, voltages, or other specific instructions, be sure to include the specific readings that are to be attained in reassembly including their units, as well as the tools and equipment necessary to attain those readings. For example: "Adjust voltage to 18VDC," not "Adjust voltage to 18." Further, if a technician is required for the operation of test equipment, be sure to list that in the document. It's not enough to say that something must be accomplished; you must list the devices and competencies needed to accomplish the task.

Examples of properly detailed instructions

Example 1: How to sharpen the blade on your rotary mower

> ATTENTION: These instructions are fictional and written for this book only.
>   Do Not Follow Them To Work On An Actual Mower

The blade your Fictional Gasoline Powered Lawn Mower will become dull after use and require sharpening.

Attention: Your Fictional mower is equipped with a gasoline-powered engine and may start when the blade is moved by hand. This can result in death or serious injury.

Remove the spark plug before proceeding.
Wear heavy gloves and safety glasses.

Read these instructions completely before you begin. Be sure that you understand them and that you have the required tools to remove the spark plug and the blade, to sharpen the blade, and to reinstall the blade and spark plug. Under no circumstances should you go forward if any step is not crystal clear to you. This mower will be dangerous to you and others if this is not done correctly. A loose or improperly tightened blade and cause severe injury or death. **Do not start the engine until you are absolutely sure that the blade is properly tightened when it is reinstalled.**

You will need:

1. Heavy gloves and safety glasses.
2. A 13/16-inch wrench to remove the spark plug.
3. A support, or assistant, to hold the mower up while you remove the blade.
4. A wooden block approximately two inches by three two inches by six inches to wedge the blade against the body of the mower.
5. A 7/8-inch wrench to remove the nut securing the blade to the mower.
6. A shop vise to hold the blade.
7. A heavy file or blade grinder.
8. A screwdriver or other circular metal shaft to be used for balancing the blade.

Procedure:

A. Be sure the mower's engine is not running.

B. Put on your heavy gloves and eye protection.

C. Remove the spark plug wire and, using the 13/16-inch wrench, remove the spark plug so that the mower cannot start. Also, removing the spark plug will make it easier for you to rotate the blade.

D. Lift and support the mower.

E. Using the wooden block wedge the blade against the body of the mower. This holds the blade so you can remove the bolt holding the blade to the mower.

F. Wearing heavy gloves, use the 7/8-inch wrench to remove the nut and washer that secures the blade to the mower.

G. Carefully place the 7/8-inch nut and washer aside; you will need them later to reinstall the blade.

H. Wearing safety glasses and your heavy gloves, place the blade in a shop vise and sharpen with a file or grinder. The cutting edge should be about 1/64-inch in thickness.

I. Check the balance of the blade by removing it from the vise and hanging it on a round shaft. (A screwdriver works fine.) Should the blade be out of balance the heavy side will sink lower than the light side. Grind or file the lower side (heavy side). Repeat until the blade hangs roughly horizontal.

J. Reinstall the blade finger tight, then using the wooden wedge tighten securely. If you are unsure of how to accomplish this, get help. **Do not start the engine until you are absolutely sure that the blade is properly tightened. An improperly tightened blade can result in severe injury or death.**

K. Remove the box or have your assistant put the mower down.

L. Reinstall spark plug and spark plug wire.

We intentionally used numbers to list the equipment and letters for the procedure. This way the user can readily see where one ends and the other begins. Further, the user will not inadvertently read the equipment list when looking for the next step in the procedure. As rotary lawn mowers are dangerous in the real world, we begin the instructions by telling the user to read the instructions all the way through before starting the job. What we want most to avoid is to have someone not be able to competently reinstall the blade and then start the engine with the blade loose. This could kill somebody. Rotary lawn mowers are nothing to toy with. So, it is vital that the user be strong enough, able enough, and competent enough, and have the tools to tighten the blade securely.

Example 2: For a non-working computer

Note: Some computer equipment on and off switches do not read On or Off. Instead they list a zero (0) and a one (1). The one (1) is the On position and the zero (0) is the Off position.

1. Verify that the electric supply to the room is adequate and functioning. To test this, plug in a lamp that you know works and turn it on. If the lamp lights and is as bright as it should be, your electric supply is working. Unplug and remove the lamp.

2. Plug your computer into the wall outlet that you just tested with the lamp.

3. Verify that your monitor is connected to the computer's video-out port and that the monitor has power from a wall socket and is turned on.

4. Verify that your keyboard and mouse are plugged in. If wireless, verify that their batteries are good and are properly installed, and that these devices are turned on.

5. Turn on the computer.

6. Turn on the monitor.

7. Wait two minutes.

8. If no response, call 1-800-PhoneNumber.

These instructions verify that the user has a working electrical connection. Many people overlook this and simply assume that their electricity is working. We've heard of a user who called for help when his building had no power. This means that you must literally spell everything out. Assume nothing when dealing with equipment that can be expected to be in the hands of a novice.

It is humorous to note that when we first heard the story of the user calling for help when the building had no power, it supposedly involved an actual technician and a user calling for assistance to get the PC working. When asked if the PC was plugged in, the user said that he could not determine if it was or not. When asked why, the user responded that the lights were out and that he could not see in the dark. The technician reportedly said something like, "You're too stupid to have a computer," or words to that effect.

There are two messages here for us—one obvious, the other less so. Never use condescending language or the like when you write. And second, write instructions for the user who truly is a novice. Assume nothing. This is hard to do because you have every right to assume that someone knows that electricity is needed for the operation of a computer. There lies the problem; you assumed. An assumption cost the American taxpayer 125 million dollars. Read about NASA and an assumption that lost a mission to Mars.

Assumptions and the loss of a satellite

Here is an example that cost the loss of the 125-million-dollar Mars Climate Orbiter spacecraft in September 1999 (*www.cse.ohio-state.edu/sce/now/mars-orbiter.html*). What happened? Well, it seems one group of scientists used miles per hour and another group used kilometers per hour. The satellite was lost because of this. Why? Because people, very smart people, assumed. They did not know. They did not ask, verify, require, or stipulate. They assumed. They did not write their specification properly. When that happens, machines are lost, projects damaged, and people killed and injured. Don't even assume that a user knows that when the lights are out the computer is out. If you can do that, and write accordingly, you will be a good and competent writer because your writing will be crystal-clear prose that everyone can understand. And that literally separates the good from the not so good.

Words have consequences. Normally, we are only worried about the return on investment of those words, the click-through rate, and the conversion rate from visitor to paying customer or how much money the site produced. Write to get inside the head of the harried user, the employee who just needs to do one little thing. Even cutting one tiny corner can be dangerous. Protect people by writing for clarity and understanding. Write tight with no fluff.

Writing driving or travel directions

When you are writing directions always tell the driver what to do, how far to travel, what to look for. Couch your directions in the positive. Never write **what is not to be done.**

YES: Go to the end of the street and **turn left.**

NO: Go to the end of the street and do not turn right.

YES: Continue 1.2 miles

           Turn left on Main Street.

           At the first intersection

           Turn right on Elm Street

NO: Take any left. Go to Elm Street and turn right.

Always write directions that tell the driver what to do. Remember that the driver is on unfamiliar ground or the instructions would not be needed, and that he or she may not have anyone to assist, or may be lost, in a hurry, confused, or afraid of becoming lost. Hence, the bolded text where turns are to be made.

Give complete directions from the North, the South, the East, and the West. Resist the temptation to lump everything in one large, terrible, chunk of impenetrable text. And never refer the user elsewhere. You know, those instructions that say something like: From the North Take Interstate 91 South to Interstate 84 and follow instructions from the East. Gee, thanks. Now the user has to go elsewhere and begin reading again. Give complete directions in their entirety.

Content that raises money for a charity

Your client needs money and is going to use the Web to raise it. That puts you in the hot seat because it is the quality of the message—your message—that either brings home the bucks or does not bring home the bucks. Here are some success strategies.

Feelings inspire people to act, to donate. Think about the TV ads that raise money. Do they talk about the millions of people in need? Never; what could any of us do to help millions of people? Nothing, but we can help one person. You, and those around you, can each help one person. You can feed and educate one person. And therein lies your success. You want readers to engage their emotions. Bringing the user's calculating brain into the mix is counterproductive to your goal. It is the user's emotions that will generate your donation.

In their excellent book, *Made to Stick*, Dan Heath and Chip Heath relate several stories about raising funds and how people make decisions. While these stories are beyond the scope of this book, the writing is not, and so we will discuss this from a writer's point of view. You want to keep the focus of the user on one person, be it a child or other worthy and needy soul that your organization is trying to help. Here, pictures, or better yet video, will assist greatly.

Content That Sells

"One must be able to express himself briefly, clearly, and convincingly, just as a salesman must."

—Claude Hopkins, Scientific Advertising

3

When the Web site you are writing for is a strategic business tool and your client's livelihood is directly connected with the site's ability to make a buck, the client will be most interested in content. One of the best things you can do is make the site a tool for the client's customers. While this is likely beyond your involvement as a writer, you can certainly suggest ways to do this to the Web master and the client. Some ways are to offer pertinent targeted news related to the product or industry, information on advancements in technology, or product tips and perhaps technical material, so that when customers have a problem, this site is the first place they turn to for help.

Offer free content. An excellent way to do this is in the form of portable document format (PDF) files. You can create them and structure them to cover the most popular products and most common questions. Another good thing is an extensive FAQ, videos, and maybe podcasts as well. To see a site with excellent information, search capability, and the ability to choose topics, products, and languages, see the Linksys technical support pages, *www.linksys.custhelp.com.* This site is truly superb, excellent technically, and is well written, and what you need can be located in numerous ways. Using multiple paths to find information is not to be minimized, as people think and search differently. To be seen as a resource when users have a problem is high praise indeed and enhances the worth of product(s) because professionals and novices alike need technical data to make your product function. Giving excellent service and access to data can spell the difference in the decision of why your product is purchased over your competition's. Those who buy, install, and maintain your products will know that you are there for them.

This alone will have your products recommended because the technicians who must do maintenance know that they can go to your Web site and get the information they need to keep the product(s) working. While true for just about anything, this is vital for complex devices.

Make the Web site a destination. A site that does this is Amazon.com. How many times have you gone there for information on a book or product? Did you then buy the product? You probably did. Amazon also provides product reviews, access to used goods, free shipping if you meet their requirements, and a powerful search engine.

To gain trust. When buying online, people need to be confident that you have the goods, will ship in a timely manner, and can be trusted to provide merchandise in the condition advertised. When customers have problems don't hide the ability for them to contact you. Some businesses actively avoid customer complaints by burying the link to their complaint department somewhere on an unrelated page. This is a mistake and lousy customer service. Place a link for those who have a problem where it can be found on the Contact Us page. You won't call it the complaint department, of course, but you can title the link something like Having a problem? or simply Contact us with questions or problems. Customers with problems will not go away and are best dealt with in an open and honest way.

Availability of customer service. Will the phone be answered by someone in the same country as the caller? Or is it answered by someone half the world away who barely speaks English? When our Dell computer needed help we were connected to fantastic customer service in the United States. Our experience with foreign customer service has been erratic. One woman was so bad that we had to continually tell her that she was doing fine, to literally raise her morale, so that she could do her job (to read the solution from her computer screen). She was not doing fine. This is not good customer service, but exists only because it is a low-cost solution. Some companies are training people to speak without an accent so that you, the caller, won't know who you are talking with. This won't make up for the lack of technical expertise, but hey, you aren't supposed to be smart enough to know that.

Just how good are these people? This is important with complex products such as computers, test equipment, automobiles, software, and networking, or something as simple as a kitchen water faucet. Recently our Delta kitchen faucet needed to be rebuilt. It came with a lifetime guarantee. A single phone call took us to a competent American who sent us the parts for free. Superb customer service by a competent English-speaking American. This is not to say that outsourcing can't be a positive experience, however, we will buy their products again without hesitation, even if they are more expensive than the competition. People will spend the extra money to buy competent service.

The availability of replacement parts, manuals, and tools, and the ability to locate and obtain them is important. Our Case garden tractor needed major work, parts, and service. One call to their customer service people found uncommon expertise. The man we talked to gave us real-time parts availability and e-mailed us several PDF files. We have never encountered better customer service anywhere. Knowledgeable, helpful, not-in-a-rush-to-dump-the-call customer service is worth paying for. While you will have no control over where customer service is located, you may be writing the instructions that they will be reading.

Methods of payment. Credit cards are ubiquitous, of course. Also consider accepting PayPal. When we sold an article to a newsletter in London, England, payment was made via PayPal. The money was transferred internationally without a problem.

Search capability. People love search capability on a site. Many problems can be avoided by simply including search capability. You can use Google to do this for you. (See Appendix J.) However, be advised that for the Google option to function, Google must first visit and index your site. When you add material to the Web site, it will not appear in Google's search results until the Google robot has revisited and re-indexed your updated site. Having said that, it works great—once your site has been visited.

Your writing must stand on its own. Do not expect the user to somehow know what you are referring to, and do not expect that the user has read material on another Web page. On the Web a user can easily find a page without having read any previous material. Calls and e-mails that report problems with a page being understood need to be taken seriously and fixed. Customer feedback must not be overlooked, ignored, or assumed to be from people who just don't get it. Your job as writer is to make the material easy to read, easy to understand, and easy to act upon. Failure to do this will drive business to competitors who operate an easy to use site.

Design. The design, look, feel, and content of the site can make you appear competent and trustworthy—or not. Take a look at infomercial sites that scroll on and on, giving you more and more sales hype. Besides the fact that this is terrible design, customers don't like it and will not read all of that impenetrable text. They simply will not read it because the Web is not a book. Write your Web material for the Web.

Testimonials. One of the best things you can offer customers are testimonials from people who have done business with you and enjoyed the experience. Here, too, appearance means everything. What is more meaningful?

Great. Loved doing business with you.

A. Smith, New York

or

Good price, competent staff.

Joe Customer, President XYZ Corporation

See the difference? The first testimonial could be from anyone from almost anywhere in New York State. The second is from a particular person from a specific business. A testimonial like this really and truly paints your business in a beautiful light. The people who read your testimonials aren't stupid. Bogus testimonials are worse than no testimonials at all.

One note on testimonials: Always ask for them. And be sure to tell the person you are asking that you may want to edit what they send you because, while people may enjoy doing business with you, a direct quotation may not read well. Always ask if it is okay to edit the quote. Then send it back for approval of your edit. We do not recommend publishing an edit of someone's words without their approval.

Testing. When you write sales-related information, use an opening title that will arouse interest, and be sure to have your content read and commented on. Act on those comments. The more tantalizing, different, or attractive, the better. When you list prices, the order in which they appear makes a difference. Customers will likely buy a $10 item if you show it after a $100 item and a $1,000 item. Showing the most expensive items first is the way to go. This is an old trick advertisers have used forever. Look at catalogues and online to see for yourself.

Give the user additional items to consider. Your offer will have more appeal when you include additional items rather than list one large item with bundled extras. Be sure the user knows that there are extras included at no extra cost. Always give alternatives.

People love savings. When you call attention to the amount of a discount, customers perceive that amount as earnings rather than as part of what they will be spending.

People hate surprises. When customers expect to pay $21 and do, they're much happier than when they expect to pay $20 and encounter an additional $1 charge. It's not the money itself, but people do not like surprises that are money related because it makes them question your honesty. You do not want the customer to leave. Remember: In the online world, your competition is only seconds away. Once you lose a user, you may well have lost him forever, especially when he perceives you as a dishonest seller, or indulging in "bait and switch" tactics. Online you must be painfully honest or you are out of business. It's as simple as that.

People dislike separate charges. It hurts more to pay $50, plus $100, plus $75, totaling $225. To make the payment disappear from your user's mind arrange for that $225 to be deducted automatically from expected income, as from paychecks or tax refunds or an existing account balance. Do that and the payment psychologically disappears. This is a powerful motivator to buy right now. Also, rebates are good. People see the bottom-line cost after the rebate and lose touch with the fact that they are paying full price up front.

In general, when you write advertising:

- Use fewer multi-syllabic words.

- Use short sentences, with simple sentence structure.

- Carefully consider the age, vocabulary, educational level, and occupation of your targeted customer. When you are selling to teenage males you will write far differently than when selling text books to graduate students.

- Use less jargon.

- Never use profanity. This turns people off and they won't buy your products. Always write in a manner that casts the product and your client in a favorable light. Remember that much merchandise is purchased as gifts. Do you think parents, grandparents, and other adults want to read profanity in the description of the gift they are planning to purchase for a teenager?

While we are on the subject of what not to use, don't say that something is "insane" or use trendy wording to refer to the way something operates or performs. Your audience is worldwide, countrywide, statewide, or regionwide. What may be fine for your neck of the woods may be an insult or complete nonsense somewhere else.

» Use shorter paragraphs. Be sure the opening sentence of your paragraph introduces what is covered in that paragraph.

» Use subheads and bullet points, when appropriate.

» Use white space.

» Don't require personal information in order to get something extra, for personal attention, for technical support, or to simply contact someone in the organization.

» Write summaries. Consider magazines and how they get you to read them. Below each article's title, the magazine offers a summary or teaser that draws you into the story. Jazzing up online articles with this technique pulls in readers and provides fodder for search engines. Sidebars, lists, and captions enable you to repeat keywords naturally and increase the keyword density of the page. To identify the most powerful keywords, test headlines against each other, or query buyers. Then track the responses and develop a map of how people found you and why they bought from you. This is invaluable information that is available for little more than the labor to collect it.

Give options. People like choices. Avoid a take-it-or-leave-it mentality. This is perhaps best evidenced in high-end computer sellers. Go to any of their sites and you will find that you can custom build your own computer. A good tactic is to offer goods in several price ranges. One that is low in price, one moderately priced, and the most expensive top-of-the-line item. This is particularly important for any store catering to professionals because they will pay for the best, longest-lasting item with the most options. Tell the user what the item comes with or how it is configured.

Consider these two scenarios. They both refer to the same car.

One:

The car is loaded.

This is how car salespeople talk. They mean that the car includes just about everything that is offered. You don't have to write this way, because, while fine in conversation where a person can expand on what is being said, online you can't do that. What you see is what you get online.

Two:

This beautifully maintained, one-year-old, pre-owned, low-mileage, late-model beauty wraps you in high-performance, climate-controlled luxury. At the beach, in the mountains, or at your favorite five-star restaurant, this car tells the world that you've arrived. In showroom condition; you also receive a one-year bumper-to-bumper warranty. Features include:

- A 300 horsepower, six cylinder engine
- Automatic transmission
- Air conditioning
- AM/FM stereo radio, 6 CD changer, and 300 watt, 13 speaker sound system
- Power moon roof
- Alloy wheels
- 60,000 mile radial tires
- Power windows
- Power, heated mirrors
- Power, heated seats
- Heated windshield wipers
- Fog lights

The car is referred to as pre-owned, not used. We use the term *showroom condition* to indicate like-new condition. You could also use *excellent condition*. We have listed features from the most important to the least important. To shorten the ad and to save space the Web master, or car dealer, only need to cut from the bottom.

As you can see the difference between the two descriptions is dramatic. On the Web you are using the written word, and only the written word, to get your message across. Yes, a picture is included, but the picture cannot present the wealth of information available through competent description. In high-ticket items such as automobiles, the chances of buying sight unseen require you to spell out specifically what the vehicle includes. Include enough information to generate a phone call or e-mail to get the dealer and buyer in communication. And please, impress on the dealer the importance of ensuring that e-mails are competently written and don't contain spelling errors. People in the market for high-end merchandise will judge the quality of the writing in e-mail and letters.

Example of poor-quality writing

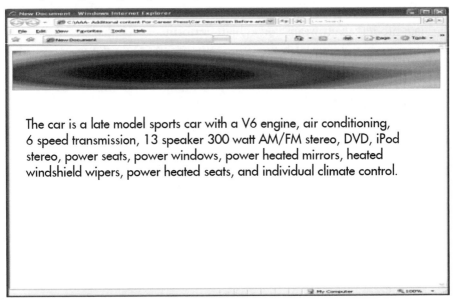

The car is a late model sports car with a V6 engine, air conditioning, 6 speed transmission, 13 speaker 300 watt AM/FM stereo, DVD, iPod stereo, power seats, power windows, power heated mirrors, heated windshield wipers, power heated seats, and individual climate control.

Example of high-quality writing

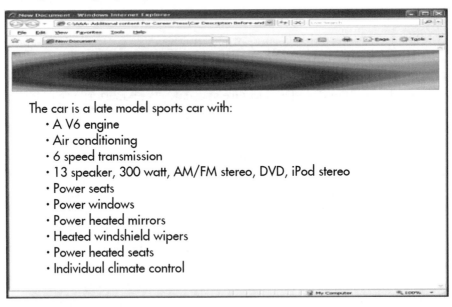

The car is a late model sports car with:
- A V6 engine
- Air conditioning
- 6 speed transmission
- 13 speaker, 300 watt, AM/FM stereo, DVD, iPod stereo
- Power seats
- Power windows
- Power heated mirrors
- Heated windshield wipers
- Power heated seats
- Individual climate control

The Psychology of Selling

There is much to say about selling and most of it will not be said here, as we are concerned with content, but it is only proper to at least touch on the high points. Indecision in others is something you can do nothing about. You can, however, move people from sitting on the fence to making a decision to buy. So, what are you going to do? You are going to allay their fears, doubts, and concerns. Fears, doubts, and concerns about what? About being cheated. About receiving inferior, counterfeit, or inferior goods and services. Do that and you are most of the way to a sale. Think about the things you buy, how you decide to buy them, and where you buy them. So what to do?

Let's start with reassurance. There is no better way to do that then with a guarantee. An unconditional, 100 percent money-back guarantee for any reason is best of all. For some reason, according to Marilyn Ross, the stronger and longer your guarantee, the fewer returns you will receive. The fewest returns come from a lifetime guarantee. Why? Buried somewhere in our head is the thought that if it thing carries a lifetime guarantee, then it must be of good quality.

Then there is the old adage "it's too good to be true." You must be sure that your sales prose do not create this opinion, because if you do no one will buy your goods. People will shy away from offers that seem too good to be true. That's a fact. When goods are offered at substandard prices, there has got to be a reason why. And most people do not want to own the item to find out what that reason is. When offering goods at a substantial discount, this must be taken into consideration to move the goods. Also, be careful of creating a situation where the customer will wait for a yearly inventory sale or other periodic low price sales event. When you need to move a product have the event you use be a one-of-a-kind non-repeatable event such as a 10-year-anniversary sale or an overstock sale. This is especially important in the online world, where you do not want to develop a reputation for the lowest price at certain times of the year. That sort of reputation can put you out of business.

Your address is important, as people will trust a street address more than a post office box. To use a post office box, place your street address above the post office box information, so you don't lose reader trust.

You will likely have need for photographs, graphics, and other images on your site. Photographs are best, as they show specifically the product and the details of that product. The user can see that nothing has been added, left out, diminished, or enhanced.

Ever heard of buyer's remorse? Ever been sorry that you bought something? What did you do? Likely you returned it. Why? Not because you did not like it, but because you simply changed your mind about the product. It was too big, too small, the wrong color, last year's model, or this year's model and last year's is cheaper. Maybe it did not offer any significant improvement, in your opinion, over something else. The reasons are legion. You need to address buyer's remorse before the sale, not later. A good way to do this is with information supplied with the product or available online. If you do not want to spend the money for an insert to be packaged with the goods, then at least provide information online where buyers can read about the product.

> Always caption your graphics and photographs. Look at these graphics. Only the bottom one tells you why it is included.
>
>
> *This graphic has a white background.*

For example, these items require after purchase input from the buyer. Think about anything with a gasoline engine that will need maintenance. Also, high-ticket items like pianos as they may need tuning or re-tuning after some time. And what about computers? Technical support is almost a necessity to keep from being deluged with machines that "don't work" because they have software problems. This type of information is not to be kept hidden if you want your products to stay in people's homes and their money in your bank account. You can also use a FAQ to this end. If you know that certain situations with products will be difficult to correct, tell the customer that up front, and put the information online as well. When people know that because of the way their product has been maintained, stored, or used that its life may be shortened, you avoid problems later on and reinforce what needs to be done to protect the product. This is also true for repairs. When the customer is informed up front that a repair may not last long, an informed decision can be made that protects you from an irate customer later.

Explain the process, the product, and the maintenance up front. Let people know what to expect before they buy. This is best for high-ticket items that need professional installation like an in-home theater. Conspicuously list the steps from initial consultation to installation. Even include financing information, if appropriate. When you and the client are on the same page, things go much smoother. And then there is the reason for the purchase. Is it to be used privately or by a business or corporation? According to Bob Bly, people would rather indulge themselves when buying for their personal use and care only that the device get the job done when buying for a business. So, when selling to consumers, appeal to their needs; when selling to a business, don't.

Encourage people to act now rather than later with these proven techniques:

❯ Limited quantities.

❯ Offer a reward or premium for those who act fast, meaning act now.

❯ Put a deadline on the price, offer, or configuration of the offer.

❯ Discount the price for fast response.

❯ Make multiple methods of response available; use e-mail, fax, telephone, and postal mail.

❯ Create a fill-in-the-blanks coupon or Web form.

❯ Make your contact information available on all e-mail, Web forms, coupons, and paperwork so your customer can easily find you.

❯ Accept credit cards, PayPal, and checks.

When you format your sales material, break it up with subheadings. This makes the material far easier to read and offers the user the advantage of knowing what comes next and facilitates finding specific information. Indent your paragraphs. This is easily done in HTML with a style sheet, if you want nonstandard indenting. Talk to your Web master. Open your paragraphs with larger-size text. This is called drop caps when used in print, and increases readership, as does indenting. Keep paragraphs to five or six sentences. Avoid like the plague solid, appearing, impenetrable blocks of text. Caption photographs and graphs. Do not expect the user to figure out why a photograph is included. Photographs and graphics must fill a need or perform a function or they will just confuse people. Never include photos without a good reason to do so. Organize your selling points with bullets or a numbered list, which is more powerful than bullets, and introduce the list with a keyword-laden heading. And never end your heading with a period. As David Ogilvy, one of the best advertising men in history, tells us, another word for a period is a *stop*. Keep columns narrow, to 40 characters or so. Any wider and they become difficult to read as users will have trouble locating the next line.

Writing eBay Advertisements

As many people who use eBay are not writers and would never hire or even think of hiring a writer, we thought that this section might be a good idea. We will discuss some techniques that work well and mention some HTML, because a little HTML can make an eBay ad really pop.

Example of eBay ad copy

First draft

high speed gaming computer for sale

desktop computer for sale for gaming includes case, power supply, 8 gig of high speed overclocked ddr2 ram, high speed fsb, 500 mb hard drive, 19 inch monitor, wireless keyboard, mouse, wireless linksys adapter, wireless router, network card with cable connector and 3 10 foot cables. us shipping included

email the gameblaster

Final draft

High Speed Gaming WinTel PC for Sale

This desktop computer is optimized for gaming. It includes:
- A 1,000 watt power supply
- 8 gigabytes of high-speed, overclocked DDR2 RAM
- A high-speed front side buss
- A 10,000 RPM, high speed, 500 MB hard drive
- A 19-inch, flat panel monitor, with 1,280 × 1,024 resolution
- A wireless keyboard
- A wireless mouse
- A wireless, Linksys adapter
- A wireless Linksys router
- Network card with cable connection and three 10-foot network cables
- Shipping to anywhere in the United States

E-mail Shawn at Shawn's Gaming Computer.

List what you are selling right up front in words that you know people will search for. You find this out by searching for similar items. Be sure to get your search terms into your ad, or it will not be found. For items that may be listed under several terms, simply place each term in your ad. If you are selling dishes, then get the word dish in the add. If the dishes are porcelain, list that.

If for a special use, be sure to say that. This is important because you want people to be able to find your specific product. To expect users to spend hours wading through thousands of ads looking for a sherbet dish is unrealistic.

When you write your ad, include some HTML to make the description a thing of beauty.

Here's a recent ad and the HTML we included.

<h1>Hasselblad Winding Crank for 500CM and Others For Manual Shutter Cocking and Film Advance

<font color="red">Compare with new Winding Cranks costing more that $100.</font></h1>

<h2>Excellent Condition.

This rapid film winding crank features a folding handle. It will serve you well. Genuine Hasselblad made in Sweden.

Email questions to <a href="mailto:Enter Your email Address Here">Wayne English</a></h2>

This offers you some advantages. Our first line is a description, which we verified at photographic sites, as this is a photographic accessory for a Hasselblad camera. Then we placed in red text that a new winder costs more than $100. Next, in <h2> heading, we listed a few words on condition. And finally, we include the e-mail address in the <a href="mailto:your email address goes here" > tag and ended the tag with a </a>.

Here is a use for your Web site that you may not have thought of: Place your eBay pictures there. You will need a link in your eBay ad to take the user to your Web site. This link will do that:

<a href=http://www.yourwebaddress.com/ebay.html target='_blank'>.

Your image tag(s) will look like this:

<img src=photo1.gif>

<img src=photo2.gif>

<img src=photo3.gif>

These three image tags will display three image files, *photo1.gif, photo2.gif,* and *photo3.gif.* Of course, these names are fictional, as is the address. You will insert the actual names of your picture files and Web address. Be sure to keep your pictures small, 2 or 3 inches by 4 or 5 inches and display them at 73 dpi. Avoid images of 300 dpi as they will be huge and take more time to render on the user's computer. In the link to your site you will see target='_blank'; this statement opens your Web site in a new window. That way, should the user close the window containing your pictures, your ad at eBay will still be onscreen.

Making high-quality pictures for your advertisement

You do not need an expensive digital camera to make high-quality photos for your ads. If you have one, so much the better, but any digital camera that will get an image into your computer will do the job. What we suggest is a simple in-home photography studio made from a white bed sheet or a towel, masking, or duct tape, an ironing board, and an iron. Be sure to read the caution below about using tape on painted walls. If you have a tripod use it, but it is not required.

Let's start with the caution on using tape on a painted wall.

You need to be very careful because you can easily pull the paint off the wall when removing the tape. That's why we suggest masking tape and not duct tape. If you use duct tape bend the tape completely over on itself and gently remove it. To avoid this all together, use a table or other surface to hold up your background.

Locate your studio near a well-lighted window or near another light source. You do want a strong light source and one that does not make a lot of shadows. Do not hesitate to combine a window with home lighting or use several lamps. Multiple sources of light will create a largely shadow-free background. The time taken to set up your studio will reward you with excellent photos.

You will use the sheet or towel as a seamless light-colored background. Pick one that is white or beige, or some other very light color. If you are photographing something that is light colored, a darker color for the background is in order so that your product does not disappear into the background. Now iron the background to remove wrinkles and fold marks. Then place the background on the support and tape it securely. Depending on the size of the background and the size of your merchandise, you may want to place the background on a table or on the floor. Now, pull the background forward and place it so there is a smooth curve where it transitions from the horizontal to vertical, and tape it securely to keep it in position. If using a tabletop, you may not need to tape the background at all. Your studio is now complete.

Place your merchandise on the background roughly half way between the edge closest to the camera and the smooth curve. Turn on your lights or open the window curtains. Your item should look great with no obvious shadows. If you have a shadow and it does not hurt the picture, leave it there. If the shadow interferes with the picture, add another light or move your existing light(s). Remember: When you stand at the camera position what you see is what the camera sees. There is no need to take test photos, and waste a lot of time to see what things look like in the camera, unless you are using the camera's flash. Just stand where you will take the picture from and look at your merchandise. Shoot a half dozen pictures and you are done with that item. Photograph additional items while you have the studio set up. Here is a professional photographer's trick: do not take the studio down until the pictures are in your computer. This way, if you need to re-photograph anything, your studio is still set up and ready to go. This is far easier and faster than setting everything up a second time.

Maximize your chance for a sale

These tips are paraphrased from the eBay Web site.

No reserve auction. Sell your goods with a no reserve auction (the minimum price that a seller is willing to accept for an item) to make getting the first bid easy. Other people are far more likely to bid once someone else has, and a reserve price can put you out of the running if your price is thought to be too high.

Shipping. Include a reasonable cost for shipping. Be careful when listing an item, in that international shipping is far more expensive that national shipping. Also be aware of the fact that the greater the distance, the more the shipping will cost. To get an estimate of your shipping charges with UPS go to *www.ups.com*. For Federal Express (FedEx) go to *www.fedex.com*.

Payment. Accepting funds online is the way to go. We use PayPal exclusively. PayPal sends you an e-mail stating who deposited the funds, how much was deposited, and when the deposit was made. Best of all, you know the money is there. PayPal charges you a fee for their services. Visit them at *www.paypal.com*. Note that when you see the additional letter *s* in their URL; it signifies a secure connection.

Description. The eBay search engine is excellent, but no search engine can find items that are mislabeled or misspelled. Include keywords that buyers will search for and verify that your description is accurate and spelled correctly.

Pictures. We've shown you how to create a serviceable studio to make high-quality pictures of your goods. Like the man said, "A picture is worth a thousand words." Use pictures to tell the story and enhance the sale. Don't forget to add pictures to your Web site and link to them from your eBay ad.

Communications. The more customer-friendly your policies are the more likely you are to convert potential buyers into loyal customers. Clearly state your returns policy in your listing. Simply by having one will increase customer confidence. If needed, include a customized FAQ on your Ask a Seller page and respond to e-mails in a timely fashion. Include extras or a handwritten note to surprise and delight your customers.

Be an expert. When your customer knows you're an expert, your ability to sell is much greater. Establish your own blog, write PDF files, and place them on your Web site to establish your bona fides and showcase your products. Establish yourself as someone who can be approached for an expert opinion. When this becomes a burden on your time, charge a fee to answer questions. People will pay for expertise. Sharing your knowledge and expertise will drive business to your site via your eBay listings and from search engines. Be sure to create About Me and My World pages to establish your presence in the eBay community.

Another thing to do online is to write posts on blogs other than your own that feature your top-selling products. When you blog be sure to leave the complete address of your eBay site and include your business e-mail address. What to blog about? Write a review of your top product.

Get free boxes, online postage, and pickup: The USPS offers a variety of free shipping supplies, which can be delivered directly to you. Also you can create and print shipping labels from your computer and schedule package pickup. This saves you money, time, and a trip to the post office.

Content That Trains

Should you become involved in training, you need to know:

1. What is it that the training is going to accomplish or what behavior will people be expected to perform after being trained?

2. How do you prove that they are able to do that?

Sounds simple, doesn't it? It's not. Hopefully your end of this will be to put the training material in Web-ready form or make the training documents themselves pretty. If you find yourself being drawn into the actual design of the program, keep these two things very much in mind; for here be dragons. Actually, it's a good idea anyway, because without knowing the goals of the training and how those goals will be tested, you can't write the program. If anyone doubts that or tells you otherwise, he or she has a major disconnect from reality. Training cannot be developed unless you know what you are training for and how you will determine if anyone is learning. Think about it; do you really want to fly on a commercial jet plane with a pilot who was never tested on taking off, flying, and landing?

We have done a great deal of training: first aid and cardiopulmonary resuscitation; Software Quality Assurance; Radiation Protection; the Mathematics, Physics and Metric Systems sections of a health physics program; and a vast amount of photography. When you write up your training program, be sure that it contains everything needed. Define all terms and list materials required—even paper and pencil. List the outcome expected and how the instructor will test, to be sure that the training was effective. Include a test in your lesson plan with the answers and verify that all answers are presented in the course. Remember that, if the students are not successful it points to the quality of the training, not to a failure on their part. You, as writer, in conjunction with the training developer, are responsible for developing and writing a program that accomplishes its stated objective. Some training is traceable by state or federal agencies. This training will include a paper trail of all items, including the lesson plan, student names, and maybe Social Security numbers, and the original tests with grade. If this is the case, be sure that the instructor is informed on how to handle the paperwork so that it gets to the proper location for archiving. It is best that this be prominently listed in the lesson plan.

The instructor's lesson plan. Instructors need special handling. Tell them if an electric outlet is needed or whether they will need a video monitor, a DVD, CD, or tape player. How long is the program expected to last in hours per class, total number of classes, and how many meetings per week? Will a white or black board be required? Will an overhead projector and screen be needed? Does the instructor need a computer with a digital overhead projector? What about special cables to connect all this technology? Be sure to include notes for the instructor to mention where the men's and ladies' rooms are located, how to find fire and emergency exits, where one can find a water fountain, where lunch will be served, if appropriate, and how best to set up the room. The instructor should not expect anyone to set up the room. In all the teaching we've done, we always arrive an hour early to get the room ready. An extension cord 25 feet long, or so, is a good thing to suggest the instructor bring along. Advise your instructors to visit the room and facility a couple of days in advance to see the room and to find where things are located. While this seems like overkill, it's not. Further, you have given your instructor(s) the information they need to be successful and so are off the hook. Should they not heed your sage advice, that is their decision. You will never hear that the training failed miserably because the instructors were not adequately briefed. Here we are not referring to computer-based training (CBT), but classroom training, which you may be asked to write and place on the Web in support of a far-flung outfit with people in numerous locations.

For CBT needs, your training will not contain instructor materials because there is no instructor. In this case, you need to ensure that the material presented does contain the answers to the questions asked and that the material and questions are written in a manner and language that are appropriate to the level of the user. Test, test, test before you put the material live on the Web. It is embarrassing for the outfit paying for the training to hear from employees that the training contained misspelled words, terrible grammar, and bad punctuation. Be sure that the training passes muster with the subject matter expert (SME). This may need to comply with state or federal regulations, and everyone in a corporation will be required to take it. When writing this type of material, having it seen and approved by knowledgeable persons is mandatory. Under no circumstances do you ever want to present to the client material that is incorrect, is dated, or does not address the latest regulations.

Training: What it is and what it isn't
Training is not education. Training gives those who are exposed to it, the ability to do something, to affect change in something, to reach a predetermined outcome with something, or to be made aware of specific material, and to attain an acceptable level of competence or knowledge. Education does not, necessarily, do that. That is why there are highly educated, highly intelligent people who can't get a job. They are educated, yes, but they are not trained. We note that many highly educated people are also highly trained, such as doctors, dentists, computer programmers, engineers, scientists, and

others as well. We do not imply that education and training are mutually exclusive. All we are saying is, you may be called upon to write up a Web-based training program. It is unlikely that you will be involved in a Web-based education program as that usually falls into the province of the instructor, the SME, the university or college or other educational institution. In the realm of education, students demand contact with their educator. The SME will take care of the technical needs of the subject matter and you, as the content writer, will likely write up or edit the course materials for the Web.

Training is specific. It is designed to impart a particular skill or information. Education is broad-based and supplies knowledge. If you doubt that, read any college course description. It tells you what will be covered. It does not tell you what you will be able to do after taking the course. That's because the goals of education and training are different.

Content for an Intranet

Intranets are Web sites available only to employees of a business. As the name implies, they are accessible from within the organization's computer system and not necessarily available to the general public. They may be of great value or totally useless, depending on the philosophy of the company. If the Intranet is used to provide high-quality company-wide information, it can be of immense benefit. One thing that can contribute mightily to the success of an Intranet is the search engine that employees use to find specific material. While search engines like Google, Yahoo, and AltaVista can be used to search a site, they may not be a good solution if you want to keep your Intranet private and hidden from the Web. In that case a search facility will need to be added to the Intranet.

As to writing for an Intranet you can use jargon because the reader knows the territory. In this case, jargon is appropriate and saves you the time and embarrassment of defining terms that users deal with every day. When placing company-confidential material on the Intranet, be absolutely sure that it is password-protected. For highly confidential information consider using a specific server and taking additional precautions. If the information is so sensitive that its release could cause devastating economic effects or other dire results, consider not placing it on the Web at all. Ever.

Some Intranets are formatted terribly, with text literally running from one side of the screen to the other. There is no need for this sort of thing. All it does is make reading difficult. If you have pages and pages of this sort of thing, check your usage statistics and see how many hits your Intranet is receiving. Part of your Intranet's job is to be presented in a manner that allows people to read and understand the material easily. Use white space, numbered and unnumbered lists, headings, and bolding of important concepts and words to make your Intranet a good one. Otherwise you are just wasting a lot of money on people, server(s), and connectivity.

Content for About Us Pages

About Us pages are found in most business sites, and writing them can be lucrative for you. This is something you will want to keep in your professional toolbox, perhaps advertise on your Web site, and maybe include on your business card as well. For sure, add it to your brochure. Here's a tip for you. Make your brochure out of heavy stock and have a perforated business card in it that can be torn out.

An About Us page has specific goals. Be careful here; remember that what you are about is passing on information that is important—to the reader. To someone likely and hopefully to be a prospective or potential client or customer. This is no place to tell everything or to write a company history. Tell the reader about the company.

» Include the benefits of doing business with the company.

» If you want to attract families, tell users that the company is a good neighbor who will be there for them when needed. That's important, especially if you offer 24-hour service. Mention the training or professional certifications that service personnel hold.

» Set the company apart from the competition in concrete, solid language. Show the user why he or she should do business with you.

» Include how long the company has been in business and the full range of products and services that are provided.

Company background and history

Even if the company is new, you can write its background by listing the accomplishments and credentials of the company's officers and senior personnel. Include where they worked, awards, patents, publications, and inventions they have received or published.

» Depending on the size of the company, you may want to include a short bio of each member of the senior staff.

➠ Listing senior management makes contacting them easy by prospective clients, if their e-mail address is included.

➠ Awards and other professional recognition are powerful and go a long way to show prospective clients that the staff has the professional qualifications to provide a prospective customer with what is needed.

➠ Remember that prospective clients need reasons to contact someone and showing that this company is well led will go a long way toward convincing people to do business there.

Content for a Newsletter

Think of a newsletter as though it is a small newspaper targeted to a specific group, industry, or technology, or slanted to a specific point of view. In fact, newspapers and leaflets are examples of newsletters. A newsletter is likely to be designed to keep the readers informed on current happenings, technology, software, and other things that are of interest to those who work in or have other interest in the area that the newsletter covers. Also, newsletters are shorter than an eZine, being only a page or two. Newsletters may be composed of many short bullets, each of which is a smattering of information on industrywide news. Newsletters hit the high spots as they are not designed for detailed, in-depth reporting on an issue. If that is required, an article can be written or referenced in the newsletter. On the Web you can include a link, but be careful using links. People want the newsletter to contain information. They do not want it to contain only links to information located elsewhere. Please note that newsletters do not need to be distributed by e-mail. Many organizations send their monthly newsletter by postal mail as well. Some even offer the choice of postal mail or e-mail. As the Web becomes more and more popular, we expect that e-mail will become the method of choice as it is far easier and cheaper.

Writing for newsletters can be lucrative for you. It is well worth adding this skill to your bag of tricks and offering your clients this service. For examples of some excellent e-mail newsletters, see the recommended sites in the section on E-mail Newsletters (starting on page 114).

Content for an eZine

An eZine is a periodic publication distributed by e-mail and likely posted on a Web site. The tendency in eZines is toward interactive content. An eZine will be structured more like a print publication, in that it will contain content that is relevant to its mission. For example, an eZine on short stories will contain short stories and perhaps articles on short story writing, plot construction, character development, dialogue, and other things that are of interest to the subscribers of the eZine.

EZine readers are knowledgeable and savvy. So, should you write for an eZine be sure that your material is pertinent, accurate, and up to date. If you have written articles for print, you can write them for an eZine. Like all writing for the Web, write tight; no fluff allowed. Be careful about including links that take the reader outside the eZine as they might not return. As in a newsletter avoid blatant advertising and marketing hype. Your readers don't want it and they should not want it there because it does not belong.

Writing Portable Document Format Files (PDFs)

Portable document format is the format created in 1993 by Adobe Systems for document exchange. The Adobe reader, available free of charge, used to view or listen to PDF files is Acrobat. You can download the latest version of Acrobat Reader at *www.adobe.com*.

These files are a fantastic way to make written or graphical information of all types available to your users. PDF files are able to be read by just about anyone, anywhere. How to create them? Your word processor can likely export what you have written to a PDF file. If that is not the case, there are third-party and Adobe software you can use to do this. When you write for an Adobe file, you do so in the same tight, no-fluff way that you write for the Web. PDF files are the perfect solution when you want to place information in a format that the user will download. They are a fantastic tool. The user can read them, print them, and even listen to them. Yes, the Adobe software will read the file to you. This is perfect for visually impaired people or someone who wants to listen to your words while he or she does something else. Acrobat can present information in different ways and search the file for specific words or phrases. To listen to a PDF using Acrobat click View, Read Out Loud.

Writing the Content

Okay, you're ready to write the material. You've met the client and perhaps talked with an employee or two. You know what kind of a company or organization they are and how they see themselves. The Web master has shown you a preliminary design and you've sat in on their meetings. You're ready to write. Begin with the keywords you will be using. If you have been asked to write the title and META tags, begin with them. For the title, craft your words so that the total number of letters and spaces is in the range of 40 to 60 characters. The title must contain pertinent keywords that will lead someone searching for them, the keywords, to the Web site. Now come the META tags, specifically the META description and META keywords tags. The description tag is a human readable sentence of a dozen words or so. The keywords tag is a comma separated list of keywords. As the site will contain more than one page, the contents of these tags can vary from page to page. This way, you cover all the needs of the site. No single page need contain all the keywords you will be using. In fact, it is in your best interest not to do this, as the more pages there are, the more chance there is that one will be found by users. With the title and META tags complete, you move on to the text that will appear on the user's monitor.

Begin with the H1 tag. This is given the most weight of all the heading tags. Be sure that it includes the keywords that are in the title and META tags. Craft your H1 tag with care because search engines will weight it heavily. Do not put words like "Welcome to our site" in heading tags; use keywords that are pertinent to the mission of this particular Web page and the mission of the entire site. This holds true for the H2 tag as well. Place related keywords that are not as important as the keywords in the H1 tag, but still heavily related to the site's mission. Remember that the H2 tag is also read by search engines. When we say that tags are read by search engines, we mean that search engines take that material into account heavily when determining if a Web page is to be included in the returns of a search.

Next in importance to search engines is bolded text. Use this for material less important than H2 tags, but still important to the site and search engines. Last is the body test itself. Write five or six sentences per paragraph, five sentences if they are a little long and six if they are a little short. As always, no fluff. Never sacrifice understanding and competent explanation for brevity. Use as many words, sentences, and paragraphs as it takes to cover the material.

Using headings and subheadings is an excellent technique. Take care that your headings do actually introduce the material that follows. While you would never make this kind of error intentionally, with the ability to cut and paste information, it is all too possible to move text and not move the heading that introduces it. This is also true for the first sentence of a paragraph. Add keywords where you can and still have the material read well. This will increase the keyword density, which is the total number of a specific keyword divided by the total words on that page. There are tools on the Web that will calculate this for you. To find one, search for keyword density calculator in your favorite search engine.

Having seen the design for the page now becomes a real benefit for you because it gives you a rough idea of just how much text you will need to fill the space allotted to content. Write and send the content to the Web master. If the design changes, you can edit the material later.

Sprinkle links in with the prose, if that is appropriate and the links have been approved. In general, links leak your ratings in search engines and can take users elsewhere, so use them with caution. When a link takes the user somewhere else in the client's site, it is not a problem. Title links appropriately. Never use: "Follow this link," "Click here for," or other such foolishness. Rather, include specific text that tells the user where the link will take him or her. Never intentionally misrepresent the destination of a link. The default on most browsers is to underline them, so refrain from underlining text. Users will think that underlined text is a link and be confused and frustrated to find that it is not. Rather, bold the information or present it in a different color.

Graphics. When photographs, graphics, charts, and tables are used be sure that they present information that enhances or makes clear what the page is dealing with. Always caption these entities. Never expect the user to figure out what a graphic is and why it is included. When using tables, place a heading at the top and, for long tables, at the bottom as well. If the table takes up more than one screen make it a scrolling table with fixed headings. (Note: Here headings refers to table headings, not H1 or H2 tags.) Nothing is worse than getting into a table and not knowing what the column refers to because the heading for that column has scrolled off the screen.

Placing print material on the Web

Many organizations simply take an article that was written for print and put it on their Web site. If you are in the business of placing your print publication on the Web, that may serve your needs, but it may not serve the reader's needs. What works for print does not work online. In general, the Web needs to be written much tighter than print does, and the Web needs white space, short paragraphs, short sentences, and headings that are designed to do the job of providing for the needs of the user and for the needs of search engines. Unaltered material written for print is not the best thing in the world to place on the Web, but it's cheap and maintains congruity with the print and online world of the organization. If you are going to do this, at least format the material for the Web. Start by removing underlined material so it will not be confused with a link. Edit paragraphs to shorten them or create more paragraphs. Pay attention to white space. Make the background white and the text color black or navy blue. Don't get cute and use color combinations that offer reduced contrast, else your users will suffer massive eyestrain.

Choosing an information format

There are numerous ways to present information. The determining factors are the needs of the user and the purpose of the content. We review several tried-and-true methods of putting your words in print or on the Web. There is no best format as needs differ.

Order of importance

This works well for information that is best presented in an ascending or descending manner. Be sure to pick what order the user will find most useful. The descending order begins with the most important item and moves on to items of lesser importance. The ascending method begins with things of lesser importance and moves on to more and more important concepts, things, or rationale. By ascending and descending we do not mean the numbers in your list, but the importance of the items on your list. Here is an example of descending order of importance:

1. The most important point.
2. The second most important point or a point of lesser importance.
3. The third most important point or a point of lesser importance than number two.
4. And so on.

When you choose this form of presentation it is important to be sure that the order is maintained throughout the list. When a list like this is edited, that's fine; when the order is changed, that's not fine.

Here is an example of ascending order that we can all relate to: your money. Let's say that you want to show readers that it is in their best interest to keep money invested for five years. You might tell your prospective investor that if they invest $1,000 at 5 percent, after five years their money will have grown to:

1st year ------------ $1,050

2 years ------------ $1,102

3 years ------------ $1,157

4 years ------------ $1,215

5 years ------------ $1,276

By using the ascending order of importance, you show clearly that, the longer the money is left invested, the more it will grow. You would never show this from the fifth year to the first year, as it would appear that the amount is getting smaller, even though you plainly indicate the years and the amounts. Showing years 5 to year 1 does not plainly show what you want it to. Be careful of how you present information.

Cause and effect

When you need to show a relationship, using cause and effect is an excellent way to do so. This technique allows you the freedom to show specific relationships and how one leads to, influences, or causes the other. When you need to show the consequences of a failure of equipment, what leads to an accident, or other consequences of an action, this is very effective. Further, you can do this in reverse and show the consequences first and then backtrack showing how the agents that caused or produced the result, accident, or effect acted. This is effective when you need to show the effects of poor maintenance or other neglect that leads to an event. In this way, you show, step by step, the chain of events and how each specifically acted to bring about the event you are analyzing.

Presenting material chronologically

This technique places information in the format of first to last in time, and is terrific for showing how things are to be done or how things have changed through time. When it is important for users to understand the order in which events take place, this is the technique to use. For added clarity, use a numbered list. Placing information in steps from first to last works well for instructions, recipes, procedures, tests, or processes, and especially when the reader will need to follow a sequence of steps. When dealing with complex material, just add more steps. Never hesitate to include everything the reader will need to know. It is better to include more material than to assume that the user already knows it. If the reader knew the material, he or she would not be reading it. See our description of how to sharpen the blade of a rotary lawn mower on page 56.

Classification

You have seen this used in science to group animals, insects, stars, students, cars, you name it. It is superb for grouping like things together and showing the similarities within the group. Here, the classification is what is important. A group may be classified in different ways for the needs of different readers. Automobiles may be classified by manufacturer, weight, miles per gallon of fuel used, popularity, performance, horsepower, or reliability. The classification will vary by what the information is intended to show or relate. In all cases, choose the classification that will be most helpful to users needs. On the Web, it is possible to construct tables that can be sorted on the fly by the user. This sort of thing can be a real asset in that the user can choose how to present information. Ask your Web master about including database capability if you want to do this.

Tables are a great way to present information. We mentioned scrolling tables. You can also make every fifth row a different color to add to ease of use, or you can simply make the entire table of a different color so it stands out visually on the screen.

In a partition

When you partition information you place information about it in terms that are important to several aspects of the device or product. For example, information on a car can be presented for salespeople, maintenance people, buyers, and even perhaps those who race the car or those who will provide after-market parts. It is the reader's purpose in needing the information that should be your guide. It is far better to partition information so that your users can easily find what they are looking for, rather than make readers wade through a vast amount of material to find what they seek. This goes a long way to making your Web site a resource for users. This will bring vast rewards in the number of users who visit your site.

Compare and contrast

Here you will show how things are the same or how they differ. You will find this useful when writing about complex topics because you can compare or contrast the topic with concepts already known to the reader. (Personal note: We use this successfully, and have for years, in our photography classes. To use knowledge that people already have in the explanation of new material is very effective.) You will need to set up the comparison or contrast in relation to the reader's knowledge and to what the reader needs to know about the new material you are presenting. Be sure to set up your material so that the comparison and contrasting is obvious. Here is an example relating to digital cameras in relation to digital single lens reflex (SLR) cameras.

	Ease of use	Availability	Accessories
Camera A			
Camera B			

This way the reader can easily see the advantages and disadvantages.

Or you can choose to list the material by cameras.

	Camera A	Camera B
Ease of use		
Availability		
Accessories		

The method you choose is determined by the message. While we have used a list to illustrate our example, this technique is not limited to list format only. It is perfect in paragraph form to show how things relate to each other or how something is created in comparison to other known processes. Here is an example of comparison that includes analogy. An analogy is a comparison of two things that are not truly similar, but that share qualities that help the reader understand the less-familiar object because that is the information, training, or thrust of your writing.

Example:

The f-stop in photography is an often misunderstood and confused concept, and that's a shame because knowledge of it can add greatly to your ability to make pictures. Think of window blinds. As you open the window blinds, more light enters the room. Closing the blinds reduces the light entering the room. Simple? Yes, of course. Well, in your camera the f-stop does the same thing as window blinds. It lets in more light when opened and less light when closed. On your lens you can find the f-stop referred to with numbers like this: 2, 2.8, 4, 5.6, 8, 11, 16, 22, and sometimes 32. As a window blind admits more light when open ½ of the way than it does when open 1/16 of the way, so too does your lens admit more light at f2 than it does at f16.

An f-stop is called an f-stop because back in the days when photography was in its infancy, lens makers literally made a piece of metal with a hole in it to control the light entering the camera. To reduce the light, smaller and smaller holes were drilled into the piece of metal. These metal devices became knows as "stops" because they stopped more and more light from entering the camera as smaller and smaller holes were selected. So, while f-stops are largely misunderstood, a knowledge of how they work and what they do will make your pictures better, because in addition to controlling the light that enters the camera they also control depth of field and that is something well worth spending time to understand.

You can see that we have used comparison, in that an f-stop is likened to a window blind, and it is safe to say that the reader does know what a window blind does. However, we still describe the action of what a window blind does and then compare this to the f-stop. We also show how the f-stop control can be identified. Next we give a short history lesson as to how the f-stop got its name and lastly mention that it determines depth of field, which, significantly, we do not explain as this is about the f-stop. Being a good writer includes knowing when to stop as well as knowing when to write. It is up to the reader to run down the information on depth of field. (Note: We have used this analogy/comparison in many photography classes. It works beautifully, making what can be a very difficult concept easily understood.) Combining techniques is very effective. Also, we use short sentences. That was not an accident. Long sentences do not enhance explanation.

Using Definitions

Defining terms is nothing new. The technique works because the user can read or ignore the material as needed, but it is there if required. You can use the informal or formal form of a definition. The informal form simply indicates what something is while the formal form indicates what group the term belongs to and what special features it has. For an example of formal definition see the excellent online dictionary by Merriam Webster at *www.m-w.com.* A superb resource, their definitions of words include the history, derivations, and pluralizing as well.

If you feel that the user will need more than a basic definition, add whatever it takes to provide the information. Feel free to include an example, an analogy, or any of the other techniques we list here. Whatever you do, it is imperative that the needs of the user be met. You do not want users to need additional research to understand a definition. And we do not imply that highly scientific or technical material should be understandable by a novice, but it should be understandable to the intended reader. Any novice to the field is expected to do the background research to learn the discipline. You, as a writer, are not responsible for making everything understandable to everyone—just your audience. This is nowhere more evident than in the definitions surrounding electricity, computers, and engineering.

Spatial Arrangement of Information

Here you will group material according to the physical arrangement of the subject. You may describe a device or machine from the top down for the user's ease in locating information relating to a specific part. This also makes it easier to see how parts fit together and interact with each other. This way, one can easily determine what parts need to be removed and in what order to get to a specific part, place, or action. Other ways to use this technique are from the inside out, side to side, top to bottom, bottom to top, north to south, nose to tail, wall to wall, door to door. Well, you get the idea. You literally choose a method of explanation based on the physical layout of what you are describing.

To enhance your description, include dimensions in appropriate units, with metric units in parentheses. Indicate height, width, depth, diameter, radius, mass, weight, voltage, or whatever is appropriate to the needs of the reader. Should you not be familiar with the units in question, be sure to verify their spelling and their proper abbreviation. Do not include definitions because you yourself don't recognize a unit. Only define terms that the user is not expected to know.

Revising the Content

There are many ways to revise material. You can read it backward or read it out loud. You can print the material and simply give it a good edit. Whatever method you choose, there is one thing that is good to do and one to be avoided. The good thing is to wait a day or two before you attempt revising. To revise too soon after writing is a mistake because you won't see what is there, but what you want to be there. What to avoid: reliance on your computer's spelling and grammar checker. While these tools are certainly to be used and will identify much that needs identifying, they cannot find the wrong word in the wrong place or mistakes that a human editor will find. And speaking of a human editor, having a trusted colleague or person of known editorial expertise read and comment on your words is the very best way to scour your prose for mistakes. Our favorite method is to wait a few days and then reread the material. Then after that we have it read and edited by someone else.

Your mouse is your friend, usually

Cutting and pasting has got to be the greatest asset any writer could want. How else can you move whole sections of material so easily? Have you ever done this and lost a vast amount of work? This blessing is a double-edged sword. Before you move a huge amount of material (read that as hours of work), save the file, and iterate the name. If you are currently working on a file named "customer-content," save the file as "customer-content1." That way, if you damage the file you are working on, you lose nothing. Just reopen customer-content and you are back where you were. No harm done, but skip this simple step and damage the file and you're—well let's just say you have got a lot of work to do—again. Save your work.

Note: We refer to a file name that includes a hyphen. This is for your working file name only. Do not place more than one hyphen in a file name that is to be uploaded to the Web. Search engines do not like that. Should you be wondering why we named the iterated file customer-content1, we did that so that in a sort the file named customer-content1 will appear just below customer-content. With the 1 as the last character, you can easily see which file is which.

Have you ever pasted content from your Web browser into a word processor and gotten this great, demented, disaster placed in the word-processing document? That happens because of the "behind the scenes" Web tags that are included with the text. The way to get around this is to use the Paste Special function in your word processor and insert the material as unformatted text. That leaves out all the HTML tags, and your pasted text will look just fine. When you need to copy an e-mail address from the net, simply right-click it, choose the copy e-mail address option, and paste it into your document. This helps you avoid the possibility of typing it incorrectly—a real advantage, as many people like to use cute and silly spelling.

Global revision

Globally revise the entire document using your word processor's search and replace ability. Should you need to change the term "nuclear fuel" to "nuclear material" simply do a search and replace. Here again, we recommend using the Save As... function to save the file with a different name. As older files will float to the top of a file name sort, all you need do to get the newer material to the top is to invert the sort or sort by latest date. Be advised, when you use the Save As... command you do two things:

1. Save your data to a different file.
2. Make the new, i.e. different file, the active document.

Be sure to do Save As... again to get back to your original document. If you do not, when you open the first document again it will not contain all your hard work. This can be disconcerting until you realize that the second document contains all those hours of work. Then you feel better, as you climb down from the ceiling.

You will also want to back up your work. For an excellent back-up scheme see Appendix J.

Detailed revising

In this step, you will be reading and revising sentence structure and your choice of language to verify that your message is clear and presents the message that you want to convey in a tone that is appropriate to the needs of the reader. You will be looking at grammar, spelling, and punctuation. Take special care with terms that are specific to the client or the industry. If you find that you have spelled a word wrong consistently, do a search and replace on the entire file. To verify that all instances of the misspelled word were changed search for the misspelling to verify that none are found.

Revising onscreen

This is an advantage that we writers have had since 1980 or so. Sure, before that those who worked with mainframes could do onscreen revision, but for the rest of us that was not the case. Revising onscreen is something we all do. It is far easier, simpler, and faster than printing out the material and reading it, at least initially. And as to working on a typewriter, there is no comparison. Our early work was done on a typewriter but we don't miss using one.

Your computer cannot tell you that you've made an error—at least not yet, but with more and more powerful computers and software this will probably not be the case for long. The advantages of using spelling and grammar checkers and the ability to revise and revise again without needing to print the material is a tremendous asset. Use your word processor to view formatting, titles, headings, page headers, and page footers. Remember that when placing information on the Web, headers and footers will not be used. They are fine for use during your initial writing, but delete them before sending the material to the Web master. Also, be sure your material is not page numbered. Should you be writing material for the Web in the form of a PDF file, then you will use headers, footers, and page numbering because these files are a stand-alone, finished product and will not be placed within an HTML file.

Evaluating Your Content

Take a look at what you have written. Is there enough content to fully develop your point of view? Have you included enough detail so the reader understands what is being presented? Are all the names, dates, facts, phone numbers, e-mail addresses, URLs, and locations correct? Are the abbreviations for states correct, and their zip codes as well? When writing, we often use the mouse to cut and paste data from one place to another and then edit it. Many times we are in a hurry or distracted, so that the edits may not be fully complete and do not read well. Now is the time to review these things and fix them. Do all graphics contain Alt= data and a caption? If not, be sure that you provide it for the Web master. Remember: Graphics and photographs should fill a need, else they will only be confusing. Also, do not use graphics for purposes other than what they were created for. If you are going to illustrate a point, be sure that your graphic specifically shows that point or concept, not something like or similar to it. Do not expect readers to look into some corner of a graphic or photograph and discern what you are writing about. Information presented graphically, or in a photograph, must dominate the image. Be sure your graphics and photographs do that. If you wish to bone up on your photographic composition skills, read *Principles of Composition* by Andreas Feininger. Written in 1973, it remains the best book on photographic composition we've ever seen. It is also the shortest. You can get it used for about three bucks online.

Definitions revisited

When you use terms, consider defining them. On the Web a "pop-up definition" can be created like this: <a href=' ' title='Definition is placed here'>Word to be defined</a>. When the user places the mouse on the underlined Word to be defined the definition will pop up. In this case the words Definition is placed here will pop up. This is an excellent technique to use. The only drawback is that it looks just like any other Web link because it is a link that goes nowhere. To get around this, speak to the Web master and have your definition links double underlined. When working with material that contains numerous words that you would like to define, never hesitate to create a definitions page or section where you include them alphabetically. This technique is excellent and particularly welcome in scientific, technical, and procedural material. If you have never written procedures, you will find that even the format of the procedure is defined in a procedure and likely will include a definitions section.

Emphasis

Have you emphasized the important points? In our description of how to sharpen the blade on a rotary mower, we make certain and obvious the dangers associated with doing this. We emphasize that because it is critically important to the life and safety of the operator of the mower. This emphasis is not to be glossed over. While emphasis for the purpose of clarity may not always be a life-and-death issue, it is needed to make things understandable. Read your material for clarity. Does your content make easily understood the important points and the purpose of the work? If not, rewrite it.

Paragraphs

Is there only one concept in every paragraph, and do you introduce that concept in the opening or topic sentence? Your readers will be scanning for what they are looking for and will expect that paragraphs contain what is in the topic sentence. Do not introduce something in a paragraph and then get to it three or four paragraphs later. When you place something in the topic sentence, cover it in that paragraph.

Headings

Headings in Web content are very important. Always pick your heading for clarity and when possible have it contain one or more keywords as well. This increases the keyword density of the page and makes finding the material easier via search engines. Be sure to place your most important headings within H1 tags, and then use H2 tags. Lesser headings can be bolded. Write headings so that important words are first. If this makes a heading that seems to be in the passive voice, so be it. That's fine. This is one very important exception to the rule of not using passive voice in your writing. There are times when the rules need to be broken to create high quality content, and this is one of them.

The format of the content

Does your content look good? Is there proper white space? Do you have vast blocks of impenetrable text? This is a no-no. Are your topic sentences introducing material in that paragraph? Do your paragraphs contain five or six sentences? Are the sentences about 15 words in length? Have you defined terms? Are you consistent with how you present acronyms? Do you tell the reader what an acronym is? Do you use a consistent format for you acronyms? Do you write Federal Bureau of Investigation (FBI) and later write NASA, the National Aeronautics and Space Administration? Pick a format for your acronyms and maintain it. Readers will notice inconsistencies. Be consistent. Your content will help no one, if the user must hunt for information. Always organize your material so that users can find what they are looking for.

Acronyms

When you use acronyms, you can never be sure that your user will know what they refer to. Slove this problem by placing the definition in a "pop-up" link. When the user's mouse is placed on NASA, its definition appears like this:

NASA

<href=" title='National Aeronautics and Space Administration'>NASA</a>

Want to make your pop-up even prettier? By using the ASCII line feed character () and the non-breaking space ( ) you can make your pop-up look like this:

NASA

<a href=" title=' National Aeronautics and Space Administration '>NASA</a>

Web Versus Print

The needs of Web content are not those of print content. The Web is highly visual containing links, video, audio, color, photos, and even advertisements. In print, text is the dominant method to get your message across. Not so on the Web. That is one of the reasons we do not favor links that take the user to another site. Your user may never return. On the Web you are fighting myriad distractions, competition, music, radio stations, and more. So your content has got to be strong, targeted, easily used, and designed to provide what it says it will provide. On the Web, it is easy to be deceptive. Users know that. The users that you want to attract are getting more and more savvy. Those sites that engage in deceptive tactics to trick people into visiting them, offer users nothing but wasted time and aggravation. Never engage in deceptive tactics; when done to extort money, all you will get is a visit from the cops.

Passive voice

Writing in the active or the passive voice indicates whether the subject of the sentence performs the main action of the sentence or receives the main action of the sentence.

Active: The driver noticed the oil pressure drop.
Passive: The drop in oil pressure was noticed by the driver.

In the active voice the subject, the driver, performs the main action, noticed. In the passive voice it is the subject, oil pressure, receives the main action.

Passive voice requires more words than the active voice and on the Web using more words than necessary to convey anything is to be avoided like the plague. While you may say that this is only a word or two in this case, over an entire document this will cause hundreds or thousands of additional words that add nothing—only fluff. Don't try to get around this by eliminating words from your work to make the passive voice less wordy. The passive voice requires you to say by whom or what, by the driver, you may be tempted to leave those words out of the sentence. Doing so creates this: The drop in oil pressure was noticed. You have left out who noticed it. You have left out critical material. Who noticed the drop in oil pressure? Never force the reader to assume who or what noticed the drop in oil pressure. Was it the driver or his team? Do not omit crucial facts. Write in the active voice.

Jargon

Use it with caution or not at all. If you must use jargon, define it. Use the pop-up method if you have to, but do something so readers are given the meaning of the term. What is jargon? It is industry- or topic-specific words or phrases that those working in an industry use routinely. For example, those people who work in the computer industry routinely use RAM to refer to Random Access Memory. Look at almost any ad for a computer; its RAM is listed. That's jargon. Medical people talk about BP when they mean blood pressure. Jargon. This can also extend to equipment, materials, and specifications. If you use jargon, define it.

Sexist language

This shows a bias against women, against their competence, or against their importance. Do not write this way. While you would never intentionally include a racist or ethnic remark, many times sexist language creeps in inadvertently. Here are a few examples:

The girls in customer service.

That is sexist. Those people are not girls. They are women.

Revise the phrase to: *The customer service representatives.*

When referring to a particular woman do not write:

Mary Smith, an attractive blond, chaired the meeting.

Revise to: *Mary Smith chaired the meeting.*

Use He or She

Do you find that you write like this?

We need an experienced operator. He must....

Try this instead: *We need an experienced operator. The person must....*

When referring to a nurse, do not write:

We need to hire another nurse. She will be responsible for....

Nurses are also of the male gender.

Revise to: *We need to hire another nurse who will be responsible for....*

Using the term *he* to refer to all people is done by many writers.

Instead of this:

We are hiring a new clerk. He will work in the mail room.

Use this construction:

We are hiring a new clerk to work in the mail room.

Using Man

When you refer to mankind, using man is acceptable. As in man-hours, when you need to refer to the amount of work to accomplish a task. In this context, you can use the term *he*, as well, but you must be referring to mankind. This is not sexist; it is a reference to an individual human. We all together comprise mankind. That is humanity, and because it is not intended as a bias against women it is not sexist, in our opinion. However, not everyone may agree with that and you may want to word your material so that this ambiguity never arises.

Use concrete words—not abstract words

Do not take your users on a trip through the tulips, down the garden path, or some other such odyssey into the land of obfuscation. Words that are abstract in general refer to ideas, conditions, and qualities, not to solid concepts, and they form sentences that contain little solid information. This fools no one, any more than a speaker who attempts to pass off verbal pap in lieu of specific hard data. Rather than writing:

> *Our performance was better in 2007 than in 2006....*

write:

> *In 2007 we did 15% more business and increased our client list by 4%....*

Be specific. Use hard data. Do not pass off information that is wishy-washy, is incomplete, or forces the user to verify your data.

Gobbledygook

This is writing that is vague, pompous, longer that it needs to be, and difficult to read. It is public enemy number one on our not-to-do list. People who write this way do not care if the material will ever be of any use to anyone. And it is a good thing they don't care, because this trash is of no use to anyone except the people who wrote it, because it shows them how smart they are and how much jargon they know and, of course, the jargon is not defined. Why define it? If the reader can't figure out my oh-so-brilliant rumblings, then the reader can just leave and go where the rest of the not-so-smart people go. Look for:

❯ Jargon.

❯ Words that are longer than necessary. For instance: *utilization*, when *use* is far better; *interface*, when *meet with* is more descriptive; *marginalize*, when *ignored* describes this far better; and other multi-syllabic intellectual treats for your reading pleasure.

❯ Flowery language. Shakespeare is famous for this and for never using five words when 10 would do. Flowery language contains more words than what are required. The words contain more syllables than what are required. On the Web, this is a disaster, because on the Web you must write tight, compact prose that accomplishes its purpose. Shakespeare was brilliant, one of the best writers ever, but he did not write for the Web. We do. Don't write like Shakespeare because not even he, we suspect, would write for the Web the way he wrote for print and stage. He was too smart for that.

Using Automated and Other People's Content

"*They are not going to read your business talk unless you make it worth their while and let the headline show it.*"

—Claude Hopkins

4

Content that is provided electronically, or in an automated way, comes to you without intervention. While this type of content will not require you to actually write it, don't feel rained on, as the client may still need your services. After all, you are the expert on the written word. To get your foot in the door never hesitate to have a short conversation with the client or Web master on what automated content is appropriate. While this may mean that you take some phone calls that you will not get paid for, hopefully this will lead to paying consulting jobs where you will design and choose automated content. At the very least, it establishes you as a Web content expert. That alone is worth the time you spend because people will call you with questions and this will lead to paying jobs.

As the name implies, this content is placed on your client's site without human intervention. Automated content is updated periodically. This includes:

- ▶ top headline news
- ▶ financial news
- ▶ the weather
- ▶ news by industry
- ▶ market information
- ▶ sports
- ▶ news by topic
- ▶ stock quotes and charts
- ▶ traffic reports for local consumption only
- ▶ customized news
- ▶ company profiles
- ▶ movie listings
- ▶ regional news
- ▶ company news
- ▶ lottery results
- ▶ news photos
- ▶ securities and exchange commission (SEC) filings
- ▶ trivia
- ▶ financial calculators
- ▶ horoscopes
- ▶ local news and things happening

This has advantages and disadvantages. So think, plan, and be careful as to what you request, because you may get more than you bargained for (if you choose the wrong content or content source). On the plus side, you don't have to work to get the material. The other side of the coin is that you do not have control over what the content brings to your client's Web site. So, if you need to represent a particular point of view or political affiliation, or have any other axe to grind, choose your automated content with care. And then keep an eye on it. You want to be sure that the material that is counter to your message does not find its way onto your site. That could be embarrassing. Another thing to be aware of is the advertising that your automated content may, and likely will, present to your users. That, too, you will need to keep an eye on and, we suggest, ask about before you select the automated content. Should a user of yours want to find something that your automated content provider placed on your Web site, you need to be aware that it may not be possible to find the particular item again—ever. Should you be asked about locating something, be sure to tell the user that the content was not provided by you, but is an automated service provided by others. Be sure that you have available an e-mail address with which the user can follow up with. We once contacted CNN about a short piece they ran, and they could not even find it, let alone tell us where they got it. That is why we suggest you get an e-mail address to refer questions and comments to for each content provider that places data on a site. One way or the other, we do not suggest that you tell a customer that you will run down the information. If you find yourself saying, "How hard can it be?" That is one question you do not want the answer to. Let your customer contact the content provider.

Before we leave this topic, let's just chat about design, your business, and the kind of automated content that will do your client the most good. Any site, whether a pizza shop or an online store, profits from having the site become a tool for users. If you want local people to buy your pizza, include links to local movie houses, the local theater, and local happenings. Make your site a tool that can be used by your customers to keep abreast of what is going on in the community. Include national and international news? Sure, of course. By the same token, if you operate a technology sales site, have links to technical news, electronic gadgets, and new equipment on the horizon that may interest your customers. This will get them thinking about buying the new goods. Don't hesitate to tout the benefits of the new gear and if possible quote a recognized expert in the field when that quote is good for your business. You might even include a link that will set your site as the user's default site on their Web browser. That way when they open their browser, your site will come up automatically. For code on setting a Web site as the user's home page or to add it to the user's favorites list, see Appendix C, Enhancements.

Copyright, Open Content, and Copyleft

Before we get into using content created by others, it is important for your legal well being and peace of mind to go into what can and cannot be legally used on your site. A good idea, don't you think?

Copyright: What it is and what it is not

Copyright is much misunderstood. The symbol for copyright is ©. Whenever you see the word or symbol it means that the material is copyrighted and to use it you are required to obtain permission from the person who owns the copyright. There are exceptions and we will discuss them. A copyright is granted to the creator of a work, whether that work is written, drawn, or spoken, a song, a newspaper column, a magazine article, or a book—upon creation of the work. These words that you are reading are copyrighted as they are being written. The creator of a work need do nothing to hold the copyright. Copyright is automatic. If you do not see a copyright notice attached to a work, that does not mean that there is not a copyright on the material.

Many people, particularly editors and others who pay writers, feel that they own the writing for which they pay. That is not necessarily true. Usually, editors and others are paying for the right to publish the material in a defined manner. Unless specific actions are taken to purchase the copyright, it—the copyright—remains with the author or creator of the work. Just because money is paid to the creator of a work does not necessarily mean that the rights to that work have been sold in their entirety. Many times, all that is purchased is the right to publish the work. Authors and other creators of work do not want to sell the copyright because all further money made from the work flows to the holder of the copyright, not to the creator.

Okay, so the copyright protects the creator from having a work stolen or used without the permission of the creator. This also keeps the money made by a work going to the creator as long as the creator holds the copyright. This can be a vast amount of money. Think Harry Potter or The Lord of the Rings. Serious money.

Look at it this way. You are reading this book. Suppose you say, "Hey I can sell this." And you proceed to do just that. You have the book published in quantity, put your name on it, and sell a million copies. You have literally stolen our property and made money from your theft. This book is intellectual property, and we hold the rights to publish it. Our copyright on this book is proof positive that it is our property. It is not yours and will never be yours to make money from. When you purchased the book you did not purchase the rights to publish the book as your own. The same holds true when you purchase a music album. You may not copy and sell it as your own. That is piracy, and you can be prosecuted for breaking the law. When anyone sells copyrighted material without permission, that's theft.

Open content

This is material that is freely available and that can be altered, changed, or edited legally. It comes from the open software initiative. Open content is material that is intended to be free of charge for everyone. Literally, for universal use. For more information see *www.opencontentalliance.org*. These people are "building a digital archive of global content for universal access." To be more correct, "The term 'Open Content' is used for creative works which are published without or at least under alleviated copyright restrictions." This definition is from *www.share.uni-koeln.de/?q=en/glossary/29*.

So, when you use open content, you are using material that is allowed to be used for its stated purpose. That means that you get high quality material at no cost.

Here are three links that you can see to acquire content.

Creative Commons: *http://creativecommons.org*

Open Content List: *http://www.opencontentlist.com*

Open Directory Project: *http://dmoz.org*

Copyleft

Generally, copyright law gives the author of a work the ability to prohibit other people or organizations from copying in any way, medium, or technology, or to distribute copies of the author's work. Copyleft allows an author to give every person who receives a copy of a work permission to reproduce, adapt, or distribute the work as long as any copies or adaptations are bound by the copyleft licensing scheme. Copyleft allows a work to be copied under a set of specific circumstances, as long as those circumstances are adhered to by the persons doing the copying. Break the agreement and there may be a bear coming to look for you. It won't be a friendly bear either.

Look at it this way: Let's say you want this book to be distributed to your employees and want to use e-mail to do so. So, we agree to do that. We send you a file containing the information that you are allowed to copy and distribute to your employees for the purposes as agreed to in our copyleft agreement. That is well, proper, and legal. It allows your company to copy and distribute the book to as many employees as you wish.

You do not own the work, nor are you entitled to sell, or transfer it to others. The copyright and all monies derived from the book remain with the author.

Finding Content on Web Sites and E-mail Newsletters

The following section lists the links where you can find content. Always begin with material from the highest rated sites that you can find. This way you will be associated with material of known quality. Should you find material that is not listed as available for free, simply ask the writer if you can use it. Yes, it is no more complicated than that. You can expect success if you agree to place the writer's name, e-mail address, Web site, and contact information on your Web site. This sort of thing is very valuable to writers and others who create online material. It is also a compliment to a writer when asked to have work published. For those writers who are selling material, you will likely not get it for free. In that case, you either ante up or move on. For professionally produced articles for the Web, you can expect them to be keyword-laden. This will increase traffic to your site because the article coincides with your interests or you would not be interested in using it. When the article is found, your site will also be found. This can result in additional business and increased search engine rankings, which can lead to advertising revenue or more business for you.

So let's find some articles.

- ⏵ BNET Research Center to locate articles, *www.findarticles.com*. Enter your search criteria and select Free and Premium Articles in the search box.

- ⏵ EzineHub, *www.ezinehub.com*. Here you can search by keyword, frequency, and subscribers.

- ⏵ Article City, Free Articles For Reprint, *www.articlecity.com*.

❱ Free Articles, *www.articles-hub.com.* Articles on news, travel, automotive, celebrities, self-improvement, business, and much more are available here.

❱ NEW-List, E-mail Newsletters, *www.new-list.com.* This site offers 8,782 e-mail newsletters by category.

❱ Newsletter Access, *www.newsletteraccess.com,* *www.newsletteraccess.com.* Lists itself as the largest directory of newsletters covering a wide array of topics.

❱ Tile.net, *www.tile.net,* is a source for all things Internet-related, including Usenet Newsgroups.

❱ Topica.com, *www.topica.com.* Offers you case studies, laws, case law, industry initiatives, regulations, Topica events, and downloads.

❱ Webscout, *www.webscout.com.* "Web-based index of Best of the Web reviews. Webscout includes only the Net's best Web sites, archives and discussion groups."

❱ Isnare.com, *www.isnare.com* for articles.

❱ EContent Digital Content Strategies and Resources, *www.econtentmag.com/lists breaking news.*

Government Sources

Here is one time when you can say that the government showed up and brought you less work. There are four important things to be aware of when using government content: (We are referring to the United States government.)

1. The government may still hold the copyright on material given, bequeathed, or assigned in some way to the government.

2. Material created by the National Technical Information Service (NTIS) may be protected by a five-year copyright.

3. The United States Postal Service is exempt. Their stamps cannot be taken and used. You cannot print their stamps and sell them, for example. Not ever, that's why we say that they are exempt from copyright protection. There is literally no copyright that will expire someday.

4. When the government publishes material that was privately created, those documents are protected by copyright. So, just because the government publishes something does not mean that you can use it for free. Remember that we are referring to use of the entire document.

Obtain government content here:

» FedWorld.com, *www.fedworld.com/.*

» The United States Government Printing Office, *www.gpoaccess.gov.*

» The Library of Congress, *www.loc.gov/rr/news/extgovd.html.* This link takes you to the Newspaper and Current Periodical Reading Room. To access the main page, go to *www.loc.gov.*

» The Central Intelligence Agency, *www.foia.cia.gov.* This takes you to their Electronic Reading Room. We also like their World Fact Book at *www.cia.gov/library/publications/the-world-factbook.* To purchase information from the World Fact Book see *www.cia.gov/library/publications/the-world-factbook/docs/purchase_info.html.*

» The Department of State's Electronic Reading Room, *www.cia.gov/library/publications/the-world-factbook/docs/purchase_info.html.*

» The U.S. Historical Documents Archive, *www.ushda.org.*

» The FBI's Electronic Reading Room, *www.foia.fbi.gov.*

Note: The Web portal for the entire U.S. Government is *www.usa.gov.* This may be useless unless you have specific information needs to run down. Should you not know where to turn in this vast array of data, use Google, and other search engines, to search a specific site. See Google's Advanced Search link on their opening page.

Syndication

Syndicated material that is placed on the Net is yours to use at no cost. Authors do this because their material contains their name and a link to their site or blog. These links greatly enhance their PageRank (that's a Google term) and will make the finding of the author's site easier. This is a good thing for any writer, and writer's of Web content are no exception. In general, you cannot change the article, remove the author information, or otherwise edit the material that you agree to use.

Syndication sites

As this is written, these sites are active in the syndication of Web content. Should these URLs not work when you read this, simply query for "content syndication" or "syndication sites" or other relevant terms. Do not use the dashes; we add them only to separate your search terms.

- Ezine Articles.com, *www.ezinearticles.com.*

- FreeSticky.com, *www.freesticky.com/stickyweb.* This site advertises 100 percent free Web site content.

- GoArticles.com, *www.goarticles.com.* Use of material is in accordance with the publisher and author guidelines.

- Purple Pages, *www.purplepages.ie/site/content/default.asp.*

- World Wide Information Outlet, *www.certificate.net.*

- Mochilla.com, *www.mochila.com.*

A note of caution: If you or your client is interested in submitting material to free content sites, we applaud your decision and suggest that you do so in PDF format with the files locked so that the material cannot be altered. There are tools to do this. A search for "lock PDF files" will reveal them. You will not need to use encryption. That is for those times that you need to send confidential data across the Net. In that case, we recommend Pretty Good Privacy, PGP, *www.pgp.com.* There are other products that will provide high-quality encryption as well. As you will be relying on this for the safety of confidential material, choose your encryption software with care. It will likely use two keys, a public key and a private key. Under no circumstances must you reveal your private key. As computers become ever more powerful, encryption will continue to evolve. Research your encryption software and be sure that it is truly secure. Security means that to break the message might take longer than the life span of the universe, certainly thousands or millions of years with current computer technology. That will change when quantum computers become available. We do not overstate this. When you or your client needs to communicate over the Net in a secure manner, the software that provides secure communication must be researched and chosen with care and understanding.

RSS feeds

By using Really Simple Syndication (RSS) technology you can access thousands of content sources. An RSS aggregator is software that takes the RSS feed and places it on a Web site. This can be technically challenging. We suggest you let competent technical help do that for you, unless, of course, you're a geek and comfortable doing this sort of stuff. One way or the other, RSS feeds are a rich source of constantly up-to-date material.

E-mail

E-mail Marketing

E-mail is the true killer app (application) of the Web and the Internet. E-mail is incredibly useful and has become a communications and marketing vehicle par excellence. Here are some reasons why you should include e-mail marketing in your list of services:

» You are a writer; you already have the ability to do this. Whether you choose plain text e-mail or HTML formatting is between you and your client. If you are thinking that you don't have the technical savvy to format in HTML, you can find tools that will do this for you. Word, WordPerfect, and other high-end word processors perform this function. The tool you need may already be on your computer. Also, you can use the material in the appendices here and get the books in our reference list. Whatever method you choose, don't let this technique evade you. It is well worth adding this technique to your list of services.

» Writing eZines, newsletters, PDFs, and other e-mail distributed products will complement your current services nicely. Further, this makes you more valuable to existing clients and opens a new endeavor for you to gain new business. Be sure to add a newsletter subscription link or form to every page of your client's Web site. Always include an opt-out link on your newsletters. There is little use in sending material to people who don't want it. There are outfits out there that will manage your list(s) for a few bucks a month. This saves you from a vast amount of work.

❧ E-mail marketing provides a new and recurring stream of business. A survey of 1,500 marketing professionals indicates that 72 percent planned to increase their spending on e-mail marketing in 2007, but more than half were outsourcing their e-mail marketing to designers and creative agencies. The work is out there.

❧ It works. Think of Buy.com and Amazon.com, just to mention two very successful sites. E-mail marketing is very cost-effective. While the cost of creation is comparable to that of direct mail, the cost of delivery is far less, as there are no printing costs, no postage, and no trucking of paper to the post office. And the response is immediate. Your customer reads the e-mail, clicks on a link, and buys the product. The majority of recipients will see the message within 24 to 48 hours. Just click and buy. And you are dealing with previous customers—preaching to the choir as it were. Any advertising person will tell you motivating an existing customer to buy is far easier than finding a new customer. When you add in demographics, past purchases, and the success rate of past advertising campaigns, you make this even more targeted, a real sales-generating machine. And, perhaps best of all—for you— the measurements generated will make all future advertising more effective. This information gained from these e-mail sales campaigns is important and not to be minimized. It is real-world data from a specific target population: your customers. The data is free, as a benefit of your e-mail campaign. Use it wisely; everyone else does.

Making Your Business E-mail More Effective

Why do we mention e-mail in relation to content? Because it contains text and people read it. Trouble is that many people simply send messages that contain little or no information relating to the message they are responding to. Consider messages like this:

Thank you.

or

Gee, that's nice.

or

I'll be sure to do that.

Thanks for what? What's nice? Be sure to do what? Aren't these responses useless? They're worse, as they refer to nothing and the reader is forced to figure out to what the sender is referring. As you likely send lots of e-mail, it is far better to include enough information so that you can figure out to what the reply is referring. As you may have suspected, we have some suggestions. Create a template for the way you answer e-mail. We use something like this:

> Today's date
>
> Name of recipient
>
> The recipient's e-mail address
>
> RE: (Regarding) A few words as to what the e-mail contains
>
> The body of the e-mail
>
> Your name
>
> Your title
>
> Your business name
>
> Your e-mail address
>
> Your Web address

You may think that some of this is redundant. It is not. Why? Should your e-mail be printed to hard copy, it is in your best interest that it be able to stand alone and that it be able to be put down and picked up and be read and make sense to someone who has not seen it before and may not be up to speed with the issue, problem, or product being discussed. To reiterate:

1. Put the date at the top of the e-mail.

2. The name of the person you are sending the e-mail to.

3. The person's e-mail address.

4. RE: (Regarding) Write a few words to indicate what the e-mail is referring to, why it is being sent, or other meaningful explanation as to why it is important for the recipient to read it.

5. The body of the e-mail.

6. Sign with your name.

7. Include your job title.

8. The name of your business.

9. Your e-mail address.

10. Your phone, fax, cell.

11. Your Web address.

What you have here is a premiere business communication format that leaves nothing to chance. This ensures that:

» E-mails you send to this person can be printed out and still easily be placed in date order.

» The recipient's name, title, company, and e-mail address are in your e-mail. This can save you should you lose an e-mail address and need to contact the person in question as all you need do is search the Sent folder of your e-mail software.

» The reason for the e-mail is clearly evident.

» The body. Here is your spell-checked text. Give it a second and third read so that you have no incorrect words. One site lists an Easter menu where they advertise "decedent" desserts. *Decedent* refers to deceased persons. What the writer intended was the word *decadent,* meaning characterized or appealing to self-indulgence. At least, let's hope so.

   An error of a single letter can make you look silly. Your spell-checker may not flag it because the word is spelled correctly; it is simply not the word you intended.

» Your name, company, e-mail address, telephone contact information, and Web site address are clearly included. This ensures that you can always be contacted. Wherever this e-mail is forwarded to it will always and forever contain your full and complete contact information. For icing on the cake, include your snail-mail address as well.

   The good thing is that you can largely automate the entire process by creating an e-mail signature. Your signature will be automatically added to every e-mail you send, saving you a lot of work and ensuring that the people you e-mail can get back to you. That's a good thing.

Software for Bulk Mailing

There are services on the Web that will provide you bulk e-mailing capability and do a wonderful job at it. Would you believe you can use Microsoft Outlook Express to get started? You can, but it will be labor-intensive. You will want to make a Mailing List that will contain the e-mail addresses, names, and other data that you care to include. Open Outlook Express, open Address Book, click New, and choose New Group. Now add all the people you want to mass mail. This can be tedious work. By that we mean it can take hours and hours of time that you could spend doing other things. For a customer list of 50 or a hundred entries it won't be too bad. For more than that you may want to schedule an hour here and an hour there until you have the list complete. Be sure to go no more than 10 minutes or so between saves.

Now, when you want to e-mail everyone on the list, simply click on the list and it will open an e-mail window where you can cut and paste your message. Do not mail it just yet. Now cut your e-mail list from the *To* line and paste it into the *bcc* line. This way your recipients will not see the contents of the list. You will need to send the e-mail to an address in the *To* line or you can't send it, so send it to yourself and you and everyone on the list will receive the message. As time goes on the addresses will go out of date and you will get notices back of undeliverable e-mail. Update the addresses that are bad and save the list.

You can also purchase e-mail lists. This cuts both ways as the list begins going out of date the day you get it. For large jobs it is likely best to have it done to have access to up-to-date e-mail addresses and save all that work.

How to insert material into the subject, body, and cc sections of an e-mail

Here is an HTML tag that will fill in the subject line of an e-mail for you and, if you wish, and add text the body of the e-mail as well.

The complete e-mail tag is shown here:

```
<a href='mailto:you@email.com?subject=Subject Material Goes
Here&body=Material here will appear in the body of the
email.&cc=ccmail@email.com'> Mail Us</a>
```

Take note of "?subject=" it places text in the subject header, "&body=" places text in the body of the e-mail, and "&cc" fills in the cc e-mail address. This sends a copy of the e-mail to the address contained there. This creates a very acceptable e-mail for your users to fill in. And it solves problems, in that you have already started the e-mail for your client. Also, your cc is filled in. This is good for comments related to the Web site as you as well as the Web master are informed of them. This way, the Web master is aware of comments, complaints, and suggestions about the site and he or she is aware that you are aware of them, too. You can use this in conjunction with the sunspammable e-mail code (see Appendix H).

Marketing using e-mail

We are not referring to spam here. We are referring to using e-mail to stay in touch with customers and clients on a regular basis, to notify of upcoming events, sales, classes, or important information about your business, or industry. And, of course, for a newsletter. This is particularly valuable for those customers who gave you permission to contact them and are interested in your information. E-mail is the perfect vehicle for this type of communication. It is fast, cheap, and easy to create and send by using a mailing list. What is a mailing list? It is a list of names and e-mail addresses that you save in your e-mail software. You can have numerous lists saved and appropriately named on your hard drive, and backed up of course.

Here are a few comments on the technique of e-mail marketing. Do not use a graphic for your header, for links, or for other important data. Graphics are not a good idea because they can be slow to download, they may not render well on the user's system, and your user may have images turned off. People turn off images to make their Web and e-mail response faster and some e-mail software has images off by default. Major ISPs block images as well. Write your e-mail in simple text, without formatting, and include a text-based link to a Web-based version of the e-mail at the top of the text-based e-mail.

For those whose e-mail software requires your address to be in their address book for access, you will simply need to get listed there by mentioning this on the subscription page. Make that easy to do by mentioning that on the subscription page when the user signs up, on every e-mail you send out, and in your confirmation e-mail as well.

When you send your e-mail always use the bcc, blind carbon copy, feature in your e-mail software. This will hide the addresses in the list from recipients. Otherwise, each and every recipient on your list will see the addresses. This will not make your customers happy. So use e-mail, but use it carefully and thoughtfully. Do this for all of your professional e-mailing.

State your privacy policy

People like to know that their e-mail and personal information will not be shared with others. State in no incertain terms that you will not share, sell, or convey in any form the information that they give you. When you use a third party to manage your newsletter be sure that you verify the policy of the people you hire to manage your e-mail list. It is imperative that you keep to your stated policy, else you will lose all trust with your clients.

E-mail newsletters

Newsletters are an opportunity for you to gain new clients and stay in touch with existing clients, and newsletters can be lucrative. The following are some of the best we've seen. Newsletters can generate sales, inform people of industry events, news, technological advancements, and new products, or simply keep your name in front of people. If you are thinking that it is a great deal of trouble keeping your mailing list up to date and offering an opt-out link, you're right—it is. To alleviate this, outsource the job. To find businesses to handle the administrative details, search for newsletter management, mass e-mail software, or newsletter list management in your favorite search engine. These services will free you from the details of adding and removing e-mail addresses from a list. However, if you wish to do your own maintenance you can do that. Microsoft Outlook allows you to create a group, name it, and maintain it. For small groups this is not a bad solution; however should your newsletter garner hundreds or thousands of members, this will become a real problem and take up valuable time.

Keep your newsletter short: no more than two pages or roughly 350 to 400 words, including your header and footer. If you have too much material for a single issue, save it for your next newsletter. If the material is truly important and you need to get into the public domain, refer to it in the newsletter and link to it on your Web site. This is an e-mail publication and it can easily contain links, video, graphics, and audio. Adding a link to material stored elsewhere is easy, viable, and an effective way to make the additional material available while keeping the newsletter manageable. Do not expect your readers to read a 2,000-word document; they won't. In fact, it's a good idea to include the word count and time to read it in the e-mail header. Keep the writing fresh and lively to maintain reader interest. If you are writing for a select audience, and not the general public, this is a situation in which industry-speak and jargon can be successfully employed. Do not underestimate e-mail as a marketing tool. It is very effective, especially when you have been give permission to contact people.

Sales

To see an excellent sales and marketing newsletter, see Buy.com's newsletter. It is very well done and contains a wide range of goods at competitive prices. This is not a newsletter designed to inform you or to offer differing views, but a device for selling their products. Buy.com's newsletter is free of charge.

Amazon.com also uses e-mail effectively, by simply e-mailing news of products that relate to goods that their customers have purchased. They track the purchases of their customers and suggest complementary goods with a product description and, in the case of music, links where you can hear samples. This sort of advertising/marketing is inexpensive and effective for placing specifically targeted information in front of people.

Newsletters that offer professional advancement

Another favorite newsletter of ours is "Power Writing," by Daphne Grey-Grant, *www.publicationcoach.com.* Published every Tuesday, it is for those who want to make their writing better. "Power Writing" is written in a friendly engaging style. Almost never more than 500 or 600 words, it packs its message into as few words as possible. This is a necessity when writing for the online world, because, while you won't read lots of text, your readers won't either. There's a message there.

Daphne's newsletter is well designed and easy to read. When you sign up for it, a verifying e-mail is sent to you and you must follow up to activate your subscription. This protects you and verifies that you, and not some third party, requested the newsletter. This is a fine newsletter management technique that you may want to adapt. Daphne takes pains to ensure that her newsletter is written in a tight informative manner. In fact, she tells you, in the header, the word count and the time required to read it. We like that. "Power Writing" is free of charge.

Industry informational

Manny Tsoupanarias's "Fuel Cell Works," *www.fuelcellsworks.com,* uses formatting graphics and color effectively. First, the newsletter is two columns wide. The right column has a highly contrasting background color with easily read black text. Black is the preferred color for all of your text. People have been reading black text for centuries. All links are in a contrasting color and are underlined.

This is a well-written, informative newsletter for those involved with the fuel cell industry. Even though it is for energy-savvy people, Manny is careful to show what acronyms relate to. That's a good thing for you to remember in your own newsletter; just because you write for savvy people does not mean that everyone knows everything. Define unusual or rarely used acronyms. "Fuel Cell Works" is free of charge.

E-mail marketing with Outlook 6

While e-mail marketing is the thrust of this whitepaper, this can also be used with great success for scheduling service calls, client visits, automotive visits, oil changes, or heating oil deliveries. Using e-mail to contact and communicate with you clients is especially cost effective for any business that needs to deal with people who are not home during business hours.

As your Web site likely comes with many e-mail boxes, you can easily have your Web master set you up with one or many e-mail addresses. For example, you might want one for every town, zip code, or other geographic area that you work in. Or you might want one for jobbers and suppliers, and another for your customers. Think over what will benefit your business best and discuss it with your Web master.

One word of caution

It is all to easy to become what I call an e-mail slave. The last thing you want is to go home at the end of the day and spend hours answering e-mail. So, we suggest that you have computer-savvy employees, who can write and take care of your e-mail needs during business hours.

To make things easier you can write canned responses to questions that you get all the time. In fact, let these questions inform you to the contents of your online FAQ (frequently asked questions). A FAQ can relieve your staff from constantly taking phone calls and answering the same questions over and over again. The acronym, FAQ, is standard on the Web, and you can have your Web master link to it on our Web site.

Why Do E-mail Marketing?

Cost. It is super cost-effective, that means a cheap—really cheap—way to contact your customers. Your cost to do this, once you have your e-mail list up and running, is the cost of the labor to write and send you ad.

Developing an e-mail list

There are two ways to get your hands on an e-mail mailing list: buy one, or create it yourself. If you decide to purchase an e-mail list your troubles are over. If you decide to create one, you've just begun. People may give you their e-mail address just for the asking. If that works and you collect enough e-mails (say 200 or more) to make your efforts worthwhile, you're good. If you need more ways to get your clients' e-mail addresses, you can do several things:

- ❯ Run a contest where you give something away and collect customer names, mailing addresses, and e-mail addresses. This costs you the value of the prize and the time to type all the information into Microsoft Outlook 6. (More about that later.)

◆ Request your customers e-mail addresses when they buy something. If they ask why, tell them that you will be offering money-saving coupons via e-mail, or some other truthful statement.

Now that you have e-mail addresses, you need to get all of them typed into a Group in the Address Book in Outlook 6.

I have chosen Microsoft Outlook 6 because it's relatively popular. There are other products out there as well, and we are not endorsing Outlook, but only using it as an example because lots of people already have it.

Before you can make a Group containing all your customer e-mail addresses you will need to type all of the e-mail addresses into Outlook. Not a fun job, but for handling 200 or 300 e-mail addresses this will do. Should your list grow to much more than that you will want to get some professional help on the payroll.

Creating an e-mail group

All of your e-mail addresses have been added. The hardest part is behind you. Now you will create a Group that will contain them. And then you will simply send mail to the entire group simultaneously.

Let's do this:

➧ Open Outlook.

➧ At the top of the monitor you will see a button to open the Address Book. Click and open the Address Book. It looks like an open book with the word *Addresses* under it.

➧ At the top of the Address Book you can do one of three things:

1. Click the New icon and select and click New Group.
2. Click File, select New Group, and click it.
3. Hold down the control key and press the letter G key (Ctrl-G). (Whatever you choose you will open the New Group window.)

➧ Type in the name of your group. IMPORTANT: Choose a name that accurately reflects the contents of the group. For example: XYZ Business E-mail Mailing List Addresses. Whatever you name the list, make it distinctive and easily recognized for what it is. Why? You may end up with more than one list and then you will need to know rapidly and accurately what list is used for which product or service.

Adding e-mail addresses to your group

In the window where you made the Group, you will see a button on the right titled Select Members. Click it and open a window where you select the e-mail addresses that you want added to the Group that you just made.

When you are finished, take a break and have a coffee. You earned it.

Writing the e-mail

The single best advice to anyone who writes for a business is this: Have other people read it, and pay attention to what they give you for comments. Remember that you are going to be bound by the information you release, else you be accused of using bait-and-switch tactics. Or, even worse, being forced to sell something at less, maybe a lot less, than it is worth.

Here is a real-world example that I am personally aware of: A product was advertised at $200 dollars. The problem is that the picture that accompanied the product was the wrong picture. The picture in the ad was a $279 product. Yes, we sold it at $200 and had the ad taken off the Web site right quick. When I say proofread, I do not mean just the words. Have a knowledgeable person see the ad, the price, and any graphics or photographs that go with it—before you publish. After is too late.

All right. Let's talk about writing. What to do in a nutshell:

➡ Write in an interesting, uplifting manner that makes owning your product pleasurable and fun—something that your customers would love to own.

➡ Use simple words and short sentences.

➡ Write for the customer. No jargon. No slang. Do NOT attempt humor. Humor in writing can be a terrible mistake. What you think is funny may not come off that way in writing.

➡ Avoid ethnic and gender references.

➡ Tell customers what the product will do for them; do not simply recite specifications. We all listen to that most important FM radio station, WIIFM—What's In It For Me.

➡ List the price, and tell people that state sales tax applies, and if shipping and handling need to be added, say so. You must not—EVER—create false expectations that lead to a higher-than-expected selling price. This is the kiss of death to a sale.

Mythical Deluxe Toaster

Poor description:

Our toaster reaches working temperature in 4.7 seconds using 12.5 amps at 120 VAC. Its double wall construction never gets warmer than 87.9 degrees. It is chrome plated with black plastic throughout. You can vary the cook time from 6.3 to 58 seconds. Onboard thermal protection stops it from catching fire. Dimensions: 12" x 12" x 8". 120 VAC cord, 50 cm. included. Warranty.

Good description:

The Mythical Deluxe Toaster will delightfully toast four slices of bread, warm bagels, or make mouthwatering English muffins. Our "Cool Side" technology is always cool to the touch—never hot. Its functional beauty will grace any kitchen. The Mythical Deluxe Toaster will make you proud. Guaranteed. Your Mythical Deluxe Toaster is energy efficient. One year unconditional warranty. It is compact at 12 inches wide, 12 inches deep, 8 inches high. Operates on standard house current, 120 VAC.

» If possible, give people a choice. Avoid a take-it-or-leave-it advertisement.

» Include a photograph, if you wish. If you do, though, please be sure that the picture is of high quality, sharply focused, and well exposed, and that the product looks good in an appropriate setting or as a catalogue picture. Poor photographs are just awful and should not be used. You can get a picture from the manufacturer or distributor, if you need to.

A word or two on pictures. Set the resolution at 73 dots per inch (dpi). This is fine for the online world, but will print horribly. Don't make the photo overly large, because you want plenty of room for the description and the price. When writing your price, write it like this: $299. This leaves no doubt that the cost is two hundred ninety-nine dollars.

» If you take credit cards, say so. If you take personal checks, say so. If you take PayPal and sell online, say so.

» Do not assume that the customer knows things. Tell the customer all the pertinent information that he or she needs to know to come and buy your product.

❧ Always list your business name, address, town, state, and zip. Why? I once got a flyer in the mail and wanted to buy the products, but I could not because the flyer did not tell me the name of the store, where it was located, the phone number, or Web site. Yes, it's true. Give complete information. Not to do so is a big mistake.

❧ Be sure that your e-mail ads can stand alone.

Sending the e-mail

Okay, you are likely thinking that all you do is click on your list, write your e-mail, and send it. You could do that, but I don't recommend it. Why? It places your e-mail group into the *To:* field and from there everyone who receives an e-mail can determine the e-mail addresses of the group members. So, don't send out any e-mail with your list in the *To:* section of the e-mail header.

So what to do? Take your mouse and cut your e-mail Group from the *To:* position and paste it into the *bcc:* field of your e-mail header. What? You don't see bcc? We can fix that.

In you open a new e-mail message window, then click View, All Headers, and you will see the bcc field. Now cut and paste the mailing list from the *To:* field into the bcc: field. To get the e-mail to actually mail itself you will need an address in the *To:* field. Simply mail it to yourself (your full e-mail address).

Don't forget to write yourself a nice, catchy subject line so that your recipients will know it is from your business and some words relating to what the e-mail contains.

Now, send it.

You're all set. Job complete. Congratulations! You just completed your first e-mail marketing adventure. Now you wait and see how effective your e-mail is. Be sure to track the returns you get and how many sales you receive.

Analyzing your results and protecting the data

Print the e-mail and take great care to look at the words, phrases, and effectiveness of the ad. As time goes on tweak the words and record the returns. This is called market research and it is absolutely invaluable, because it is real-world, hard data from your customers.

Soon you will develop a set of words and phrases that is more effective at making sales than other words and phrases. Stay with those words and phases.

One more thing: Treat those words and phrases as company confidential information. Don't discus them with your employees, vendors, friends, family— no one. These people talk and you don't want this material to leak to your competition.

The results of your marketing campaign are best kept to yourself. This protects your best interests.

Your Blog

6

The word *blog* is a portmanteau word that comes from *Web* and *log* and can be thought of as an online diary. In this diary, you and your users do the writing. A blog has some real advantages, not the least of which is having fresh content added to it daily. The constant updating of the blog makes search engines take notice of you. Should your blog acquire substantial traffic it can be a source of revenue, because all that traffic will bring advertisers and people who will pay to read your content. Blog traffic is measured in "hits per day," meaning visits per day. It is very possible for you to use a blog to advertise your business, your point of view, or something you feel passionate about, or just to air your opinion. So, whether you want to have your say about radio-controlled vehicles, politics, or dogs, a blog will allow you to do that and do it easily, effectively, and cheaply. In fact, people are using blogs rather than Web sites because they are easily set up, requiring little technical expertise, look much like a Web site, attract visitors who make comments, and are easily maintained. And the expense of a Web master or a content writer can be avoided. We say "can be" advisedly as some blogs hire writers to provide content.

A friend of ours, Peter Crowley, uses a blog and a Web site to showcase his photography. His blog garners 4,000, or more, hits per day. Peter was a contributor to one of Nikon's publications and so had a following that he brought with him. Read about his work at *www.peterjcrowley.com/blog/index.html*. Also, notice that the address of his blog contains the address of his Web site.

For a Better Blog

There are blogs aplenty out there and vast amounts of advice on how to make your blog stand out from others. Whole books are written and there is a vast amount of information online. So, for what its worth, here's what we think.

People want opinions, so be opinionated. Do not rehash the evening news. This is no place for "maybe this" and then again "maybe that." Have the courage of your convictions and write a strong blog. Keep up to speed on developments in your area. If you are writing about politics, you simply must be well informed. If you write about radio-controlled monster trucks, you had better know the industry, what products are new, and what products are "in the pipe" awaiting release. This means research online and offline. Wherever possible, try for telephone, or in-person, interviews for truly fresh material. When you write something truly controversial, be sure to list your sources. And we mean the primary source—not what a third party reports, but the original publisher of the material. This goes to the heart of your credibility. You simply must tell people where material comes from, else you are nothing more than a rumormonger. Base your opinions on fact.

Link to supporting material and related material. Don't hesitate to include numerous links for support of your opinion. Avoid using only one link. There lies madness. Credit your sources and have more than one source. Because your first link is the main link for the article, make it an important one, as it is the one that will be followed most often. In fact, it may be the only link that your users follow. Credit your source like this: "General Motors reports..." or "According to a news item on CNN, *www.cnn.com/newsitem....*" This language builds credibility by showing that you've done your homework when you identify your source, and the user can judge the quality of that source and so the quality of your post and blog.

When you write, less is more. This simple truth is often cited and can be misunderstood all too easily. Avoid a 10,000-word novella. Keep your blog posts to 250 to 300 words. Use short, punchy sentences. And say what you've got to say in easily understood language.

Headings and headlines. These are important; make the words count. If your heading is in the passive voice, that's okay. Clarity and ease of understanding are your holy grail; be not a slave to rules. Use headlines and headings that are catchy and focused on the subject that they introduce. Headings and headlines must be spelled correctly. Never use any sort of misspelling, or cute and intentional misspelling, in a headline or heading. It will never be found by users.

Passion. Yours, write with it. Now is the time to tell and show what and how you feel, but not with vulgar, insulting, or hateful language. Make a case for your point of view that is intelligent, well thought out, and well written. No one will read material written by an ignorant lunatic. To have your opinion read it must be readable and palatable. Hate speech serves no one. Avoid vulgarity like the plague. It should and will destroy your credibility. Always seek to present yourself as an intelligent, thoughtful writer.

Structuring your words. Nothing beats a bulleted or numbered list for constructing material that is easily read, is easily found, and that just plain looks good. Use an unnumbered list when the order is not pertinent and a numbered list when the order that things happened, or must be considered, is required. Use headings to introduce material and use them liberally. Your readers will be scanning your blog and headings. Make it easy for them to find what they are looking for.

Edit your words. Do not try to write finished material on the first attempt, but do read and edit your material before you place it online. Use a word processor to do the writing and then cut and paste it into your blog. That is an excellent technique and gives you a powerful platform that includes a spelling and grammar checker, a dictionary, and a thesaurus. Word processors are designed for just this sort of thing; use one.

Pick and maintain a consistent style. When you write professionally, you need to develop and maintain a style. People will come to expect you to maintain that style. Pick up any newspaper or read news reports online. You can quickly see the way people write. Use humor carefully when you have an international audience, or not at all.

Use the inverted pyramid. Place the most important material first. In successive posts, use a few lines to introduce the user to the subject. Do not expect that your readers will have read all the background material leading up to your current work. You do, after all, want to attract new readers. Leave a trail of breadcrumbs, so the user gets the idea of the post. This is a tried-and-true technique for bringing people up to speed.

Here are some things that will make your blog better, according to Jakob Nielsen's Alertbox.

➧ Your biographical information. People like to know who is writing the blog. Include an About Us page and tell people about you. The only exception to this is for a business where personal information about the blogger is inappropriate, because readers want to know about the business.

- Include a picture of yourself. This makes your blog more personal. An added advantage is that you will be recognized by your readers. This is especially good when you speak at events related to the blog.

- The description of your links. Users want your links to reflect the information that they point to. Simple as that. Perhaps the single best way to ensure that your links are descriptive is to ask yourself if the link is general in nature or specific. Users find general titles rather nebulous, because generalization is open to interpretation and may turn out to be something other than what the user expects. Write descriptive links.

- Links that do not specifically tell where they take the user. Never write non-descriptive words such as *what people think, more*, and other words that do not inform people of what information the link relates to.

- Popular material that is difficult to find. Don't bury your successful material. Just link to it specifically or list your top 10 or top 20 posts on your blog.

- Navigation. Create your navigation in such a manner that it facilitates ease of searching and locating material. Avoid listing material by the date that it was written. There is no way that users can be expected to know this and so they have little chance of finding what they seek.

- Your publishing frequency. Are you up to date? Do you publish on a regular schedule? Most blogs are updated daily; however, it's your blog, and weekly or monthly updates are fine. Find a schedule that works for you and maintain it. This makes it far easier for your users and for you as well. With a regular publishing schedule, you choose when to work on the blog and do not get caught in time constraints or have an irregular publishing schedule.

- Stay on topic. Do not include unrelated material as this just confuses people. Worst of all, you will not attract the high-end users who will come again and again. The only people who will read such a blog are those with too much time on their hands. What you want are people who are interested in a specific topic and who choose to read your blog to maintain their knowledge base, or who value the opinions expressed on your blog.

- Your future boss. Don't forget for whom you are writing. This will be read by people who may want to employ you someday. Any material that you place on the Web can be expected to remain there forever.

- Your domain name. Having your domain owned by a service and not you is not professional, and is the mark of a beginner.

Let's move to blog addresses and subdomains, which are the professional and upscale ways to go. (We suggest that your blog address contain your Web address.)

The Environment of Your Blog

This is how your blog is presented to users. Do you want a professional feel or a friendly ambience? If you are too candid and friendly, or too cavalier, you'll turn people off if this is a professional blog. And the other side of the coin is true as well. If you make your blog too sterile, no one will want to read it. So, aim for readability. Even a professional blog can be made interesting and lively. In fact, it should be interesting and lively.

The language you use to get the message across is important. If you come across as a know-it-all, your readers will go elsewhere. Too much basic explanation is bad as well. Stay with a candid blog that reads to users as they would be spoken to in conversation. And before we forget, let's not get on our high horse, and let's not preach either. In fact, preach with caution. When you write for a small audience, you lose the vast majority of users and have no chance to influence them or introduce them to your way of thinking.

Considerations

To make your blog more interesting, invite others to write comments to gain a different perspective. This works best in a public blog and that is likely what you have in mind, but that is not the only way to go. You can create a private blog for, let's say, a large project, when you want a communications medium that is easily accessed by everyone working on the project, whether the participants are local or spread across the world. Or, of course, you can use a private blog as a subscription-only medium, to generate revenue. Either way, keep a private blog in mind, as it may be an excellent solution to a communications problem. This is especially true when your team is in different time zones as it allows continuous communications and work to go forward around the clock because one team uploads their day's work and the next team down loads it and continues.

Are you writing a book or working with an author? Use a private blog to have the book peer reviewed. This is being done and works out very well, shortening the time peer review takes, eliminating copy and postal fees, and making the review process able to proceed around the clock, worldwide, and at the convenience of the reviewers.

Creating Your Blog With TypePad or Other Professional Tools

There are many ways to obtain, set up, and manage a blog. A free-of-charge blog can be set up at *www.blogger.com*. There are advantages and disadvantages, of course. While a free blog may be fine, the services and design capabilities of the professional services are not to be underestimated. Professional blog software includes WordPress, *www.wordpress.org,* for your blog host. They have a great deal to offer. We like, use, and pay for the services offered by TypePad, *www.typepad.com.* Their Plus Level service, includes 500MB of storage and 5GB of bandwidth per month, at a cost of about $9 per month. We also wanted the ability of domain name forwarding.

To see TypePad for yourself, visit *www.typepad.com.* They have several plans and a wide array of designs, colors, fonts, and formats. One will likely suit your needs, but, if not, you can create a custom format. Their designs do include seasonal material, if you are a seasonal business. Of course, you can easily change the design after the season passes. We recommend that you use TypePad's Domain Name Forwarding feature to map the name of your blog to your Website's URL. It is more professional than having your blog's URL be something totally unrelated to your business Web address. Our blog's address is *www.blog.webcontentrx.com.* Even though the blog is actually located on TypePad's server, it is accessed via our address. Without domain mapping, the address would have been *http://webcontentrx.typepad.com/webcontentrx/.* As you can see, this address does not include our Web address. As to technical support, TypePad's people know their job and get back to you in a timely manner.

You may be wondering why we were so insistent on having the blog and Web addresses reflect each other. That is a valid question, and the answer goes to branding, search engines, and the title of this book. When anyone searches for the book title, they find the blog and our Web site. This ties the book, the blog, the Web site, everything, together. That is part of our marketing plan.

Advantages TypePad offers
➡ You may edit or delete any comment at any time. This prevents people from placing material on your blog and keeping it there. Access this by clicking on Weblogs—Select your blog—Edit an existing post.

➡ You can add images and pictures to comments. When you edit a post, simply click the Insert Image button on the toolbar. Then browse and select Use Default Settings or Use Custom Settings. Custom Settings include the ability to Wrap Text, Image on Left, Image on Right, Create Thumbnail, or Popup Window. You can also save these settings as the default.

➧ You can upload, link, and share files. For example you may want to share a whitepaper that is of wide interest. Title the whitepaper appropriately, so users will easily understand what its subject is and allow them to easily find it. For example: Whitepaper: HTML and Web 2.0 [PDF 75KB]. This title provides instant recognition, the type of file, and the size of the file. Including the file size is a good idea for those users who have a slow Internet connection. When editing a post, click the Insert File button, browse to the file, select it, and click the Upload File button.

➧ You have the ability to write a comment and schedule when it will be available to users. Also, comments can be backdated so as to appear in your archives. This is important for material that you wrote before the blog existed. This way, the material that predates the blog can appear in your archives in chronological order. Write your post in the Compose New Post: YourBlog'sName screen—then, at the bottom of the page in the Posting Status dropdown box select Publish On..., and select the date from the calendar.

➧ You have the capability to approve every comment before it is available for users. We particularly like this feature, because you can easily ensure that all comments are accurate, pertinent, and well written before the public sees them. TypePad will e-mail you when a comment requires your approval. You then simply log on and decide on how you wish to handle it. To enable Comment Approval: Weblogs—Select Your Blog—Configure—Feedback—Moderation—select Hold comments for approval.

➧ TypePad is set up to use TypeKey (*www.sixapart.com/typekey*) for comments and authentication of identity. This prevents someone from using your name in a comment. You can require this, make it optional, or turn it off all together. You can also require unauthenticated users to leave their e-mail address or go through CAPTCHA (*www.captcha.net*).

➧ The design of your blog can be changed whenever you like: Weblogs—Manage—Edit your current design.

Promoting Your Blog

Getting the word out that you have a blog is no different from any other sort of information dissemination. Use word of mouth; tell customers, clients, friends, family, and colleagues about your blog. Write a press release and send it to television, radio, and newspapers in your area. For a professional outlet that will send your press release around your state, region, or the entire country you can use PR Web, *www.prweb.com,* or another similar service. Be sure to place your Web address, blog address, and e-mail address on your business paperwork, business card, and stationery, and add it to your e-mail signature. Have magnetic mount signs made for your car doors and a decal for your back bumper that contains your online addresses. Also look up sites that provide online ads. Then have your blog indexed by blog search engines like Yahoo, *www.ysearchblog.com,* and Google, *www.blogsearch.google.com.* There are many others; they are easily found with a search.

Be sure to link to resources that are related to your blog and become a regular visitor and contributor to blogs that you like and that relate to your business. When you post a comment be sure to know what keywords people are using to search for comments like yours and be sure your post contains the URL (Universal Resource Locator—your blog's Web address) to your blog. To find what keywords are pertinent, use Google's keyword tool, *www.adwords.google.com/select/KeywordToolExternal* (*www.wordtracker.com*). Knowing the keywords that people are using is important to any post you make.

Don't forget the social networking sites. Twitter, Facebook, YouTube, and others offer a tremendous resource to get your blog, your business, and yourself known and followed. If you use Twitter, think of including your URL in the headline. For business and professional use there is LinkedIn. The networking sites offer you exposure and ways to find new business.

Attracting Traffic to Your Blog

To have people become part of your conversation, it helps if you become part of theirs. Give your blog time to become known, accepted, and found by interested people. Your blog is not a shortcut to fame and recognition, but can contribute mightily as an advertising vehicle to gain new business. A successful blog can be yours, but like most things in life it will take time and effort. Take your time; build your reputation, your brand, your base.

7

Getting Found: Content and Search Engines

In this section, we will only discuss how to optimize a Web site's text for search engines. This is not to be confused with full blown Search Engine Optimization (SEO), to achieve a specific placement in one or more specific search engines. For complete SEO services, you will want to contact an organization like Service Internet Solutions, *www.SISIntl.com*, to SEO your site, or provide you with a Search Engine Marketing and Optimization campaign. Contact them at (860) 292-1557 or e-mail solutions@sisintl.com.

A Brief Primer on Hypertext Markup Language (HTML)

Hypertext markup language, or HTML, as it is almost universally called, was designed to be easy to use and it is. If all this technical stuff is not for you, don't feel rained on; as a writer you do not need to know how to do Web stuff. We include this for those of you are interested.

- ❯ HTML instructions are called tags.

- ❯ Tags are placed between the < and > characters. For example, <center> will center all material that follows it.

- ❯ To end the action of a tag you use the tag again, but lead it with a back slash /, like this: </center> this ends the action of the center tag.

All of the tags that we talk about here will be located in a file whose name ends with the characters .htm or .html. This identifies the file to your browser as an HTML file, and your browser will interpret the tags as instructions on how to show your material onscreen. There are other kinds of browser-readable files, like active server pages (.asp) and others. We are only discussing HTML files here.

An HTML file begins with the HEAD section. Note: HTML tags can be un uppercase or lowercase. So, <H1> will have the same effect as <h1>.

<HEAD>

In the <head> section of any HTML file you will find the <title> tag, the <META> tag, and other tags. These are of concern for getting your site found by search engines and users. There are other tags in the head section as well; we will not discuss them because this is not a book on HTML.

<TITLE>

Perhaps the most important tag on any Web page, as far as search engines are concerned, is the title tag. What appears between the <TITLE> and </TITLE> is of critical importance. It is in your, and your client's, best interest that each page contains information between the <TITLE> </TITLE> tags. Be sure that the first word in the title is the most important word and specific to the needs of that particular page.

➡ Titles must be in mixed case and contain no HTML or formatting. Do not attempt to control the color or font of the title. Do not place the first word in a title in capital letters to emphasize it. Being first is sufficient.

➡ Keep your title text between 40 and 60 characters in length. The first 40 characters must describe the page, as search engines sometimes truncate the text and may not display the title text in its entirety.

➡ Never use "Welcome to [business name]." Why? For users to find your client's site they must know the business name. So you will only be found by people who already know you exist.

➡ Research words for the title with online tools like Google, *www.adwords.google.com,* and by searching on the terms that you believe will make high-quality title words. Be sure that your title words generate search engine returns that will guide users to your client's site. Use several search engines to check the effectiveness of your keywords. See Testing Your Content, on page 137.

➠ Don't place anything in the <TITLE> tag except specifically targeted words that will lead searchers to your site. Look for and remove words such as:

    ❯ Index page

    ❯ Home page

    ❯ Welcome to.... See this for yourself: Open any search engine and search "Welcome to." Google reports 786 million returns. Yahoo reports 1.9 billion. Do you want to be one of them?

    ❯ The name of your business, unless you are so well known that users can be expected to search for your business name.

META tags

The term META means that these tags are information about information. That is where the name comes from. While not as important as they were, they are still useful. To see META tags in action go to AltaVista, *www.altavista.com,* search for just about anything. The description you see about the sites returned is likely from the META description tag. Each page of a Web site needs to contain a META description tag containing 150 characters or less. Descriptions need to make sense, be readable, and describe the information found on that specific Web page.

Do not insert marketing language. META tags are used to describe the contents of the page, in terms that make sense to the reader. Never insert information in META tags that is not found on the page, in an attempt to get users to the site surreptitiously or in a deceitful manner. This is dishonest, fools no one, is deceptive, and will destroy your credibility instantly.

The META tags that are of most use to us are these:

<META name="Description" CONTENT=" " /> This is a readable sentence that describes the site. It is important to have the words here match those in the body of the page.

The <META name= "Keywords" CONTENT=" " /> tag. Here you will place keywords separated by commas. These keywords are pertinent to the page in question. It is important to realize that META tags can change from page to page on a Web site. On each page choose a META description and META keywords that are appropriate for that specific Web page. Do this for every page on a Web site. To close a META tag, so that it will be XML compatible, simply include the back slash character, /, as shown.

For example, on an About Us page you will use different information in the META tags than you use on the site's opening page. Just be sure that the information that the META tags contain is appropriate to the needs of the page on which they appear. This way, when users search for you, hopefully one of your pages will appear in the search returns and lead the user to your site.

The <H1> Heading Tag

Moving down the Web page, next we find the heading tags. Place your most important, highest rating keywords between <H1> and </H1> tags. Search engines rate the words placed here in determining your rank. Text placed between <H1> and </H1> tags is given higher relevance than words placed between <H2> and </H2> tags. So, put your most important keywords within <H1> and </H1> tags.

HTML heading tags range from <H1> to <H6>. Keep your headings not more than four deep because, as they become smaller and smaller, they are more and more difficult for users to differentiate visually. Remember: <H1> creates the largest text size and <H6> creates the smallest size text.

The <H2> Heading Tag

As in <H1>, place your next most important keywords between <H2> and </H2> tags. This tells search engines that these words are important but not as important as what is found between <H1> and </H1>.

Doing this can go a long way to having your site come up in a search. And to be found, you have got to be included in a user's search.

Bold

For those words that are important, but not as critical as <H2> level terms, you can present them in bolded text. To bold text, use the <B> tag. Like this: <b>This text would appear in bold font.</b> You can also use the <strong> tag: <strong>This text would also appear in bold.</strong>.

Why are there two tags that do the same thing? The strong tag takes numerous attributes that the bold tag does not. If all you want to do is bold your text, either will do. We always use the <B> tag. To see the attributes available with the strong tag, search for HTML strong in your favorite search engine.

Hyperlinks

Links are used for navigation within a Web site and for accessing other sites as well. Too many links to other sites will hurt you in search engine rankings. Think of outside links as leaking page rank. To increase your page rank, seek other sites that will link to you. A good way to do this is to find sites that are related to yours and link to each other. Search engines like that, because, if tens, hundreds, or thousands of sites think that your site is important enough for them to link to, then you must have a site that is important. That is why we say that your site is best viewed as a resource, because people will link to a resource. All those links are great for your placement in search engine returns. Remember now that we are not talking about bookmarks, but links from other Web sites that take the user to your site. And speaking of links, when you write the link text—that is, the words that will appear on your Web site—use as many keywords as possible. This helps with keyword density and makes your links important to the user because they relate directly to the mission of the site and to user interest.

Superior Links and How to Create Them

1. Use a double underline to indicate a definition.

   This is a definition.

   `<A href='WebAddress' style='border-bottom-style: double: border-bottom-color: black: border-bottom-width: 1px'>This is a definition.</a>`

2. Navigational links do not need to be underlined.

   Home   About Us   Contact Us

   `<A href='WebAddress' style='text-decoration: none'>Home</a>`
   `<A href='WebAddress' style='text-decoration: none'>About Us</a>`
   `<A href='WebAddress' style='text-decoration: none'>Contact Us</a>`

3. Never title links like this; they tell search engines nothing.

   Click Here to download our application for Admission

   Follow this link to see what our customers are saying about us.

   Rather:

   Download our Application for Admission Testimonials

4. Place a line on top of your link text.

   For a different look and to attract attention.

   `<A href='WebAddress' style='text-decoration: overline'>For a different look and to attract attention.</a>`

5. Make a graphic or photograph a link.

   `<A href=WebAddress><img src='name of graphic'></a>`

Bulleted Lists

Another way to call attention to keywords is with a list. Bullets are simply large dots, or other small graphics, in front of material, like this:

- This is bulleted.

On the Web, any small graphic can be used as a bullet. Ask your Web master about this if you wish to use a check mark, a ball, or some other favorite graphic. Listing is an excellent technique for presenting related information.

Finding Keywords

Think of keywords as the search criteria that people will use in search engines to find your site. They are of critical importance to your site being found by search engines. See that your site is keyword-laden, but do not exceed about 5 percent of all the words on any page for any single keyword. Search engines do not like that and may consider your site not a good one to list.

Enter words that you think people will use to find your site and these tools will return the number of searches that have been made using that term. When you find keywords that work for you, make a list of them and pack them into your Web site. Use them in the <title>, <h1>, <h2>, links, text, and the name of your files. Use them. Here, as for blogs, use Google's tool, *www.adwords.google.com*, or *www.addme.com/keywordsuggest.htm* at *AddMe.com*. There are others of course; find them by searching for keyword finder in Google. Also, look at the keywords your competition is using.

To research what the competition is using for keywords, we recommend Spyfu, *www.spyfu.com*. Spyfu will give you the Top 100 Organically Ranked Domains, the Top 100 Advertisers, and the Top 100 Most Expensive Keywords. That is the cost per click (CPC). You will also find the Top 500 Most Clicked Terms. Spyfu is very interesting and well worth a look. When searching on a keyword, or keywords, you will find the Cost/Click, Clicks/Day, and Cost/Day, and Advertisers and Search results. Further, you will find the keywords that advertisers bought, related terms, and search results. This information allows you to specifically tailor your keywords and to avoid keywords that your competitors are using. Better yet, you can take advantage of keywords that they are not using, but that are appropriate for your needs.

Would you like to know your competitors' advertising budget on the Web? Of course, who wouldn't? Spyfu will give you their daily ad budget.

You can literally compare your advertising budget to that of your competitors. There is a wealth of information available here at no cost. You can subscribe to Spyfu for 3 days, on a monthly basis, or for one year. Subscribers have access to Spyfu's Advanced Analytics, Advanced Search capability, and the ability to export data to an Excel spreadsheet. Spyfu can be an invaluable tool.

Graphics and Alt Text

When graphics are placed on a Web site you can add what is called alt= (alt equal) data within the graphic's HTML tag. This information will appear onscreen when the mouse curser is placed on the graphic. While your Web master will need to add this to the graphic tag in question, you can write up the words to be added. For your alt equals data, use words that describe the graphic. This is important when users turn off graphics capability and for those who are visually impaired.

Alt data is important if your graphics are to be found by search engines. Digital cameras can give every picture a random name—DSC0001.jpg, for example. As you can see, this name has nothing to do with the subject of the picture. So, when you place this picture on a Web site, adding pertinent information that will let a search engine index the picture is mandatory, if you want that picture to be found. Let's say the picture is that of a tricycle. To make the picture visible on a Web page and offer information to a search engine, the HTML tag might look like this: <img src=DSC0001.JPG alt='Tricycle'>. This will actually pop up the word *Tricycle* when the mouse is placed on the picture.

Keep your alt=' ' description to 10 words or fewer and be sure to use words that are related to the photograph or words that a user can be expected to search for to find the picture. To insert words like *Picnic 2007* will not be meaningful when someone wants to find the picture later. However, if you do not care if a search engine ever finds the picture, then use any words you wish, but in general keeping your description as precise, unique, and descriptive as possible is a good idea.

Testing Your Content

Test your title text by literally placing your title words into several search engines and scrutinizing the results. If the sites returned are highly relevant, then you have done your job well and your title text is fine. If not, your title may be too specific, not specific enough, or too long, or it does not express the specific topic of the Web site in terms that are meaningful to the search engine. One thing you can do is look for sites that are relevant, by studying the competition and seeing what text they are using. Then use similar material. Titles are always visible in the browser's very top bar. You need not go through a great deal of trouble to see the title. Should you want to see the HTML for any page, use the browsers View, Page Source utility. Also, search for your <H1>, <H2>, and <META> tags as well, but, because the <TITLE> text is of critical importance, concentrate on that. When you find relevant words, be sure that they appear in your title, and never hesitate to have different words in the <TITLE> tag of every page in your site. That way, you cover all your bases and have the greatest chance of one of your pages being found. It is getting found that you are concentrating on with your <TITLE> text.

Here is an example relating to one of our clients, a hotelier in Misquamicut, Rhode Island, who operated three hotels. We updated her site, and the increase in telephone traffic was so drastic that we were asked to take the changes down. The employees could not keep up with the phone calls. By carefully analyzing the keywords of the competition you can make a dramatic contribution to your client's success.

Search Engines, E-mail, and the Web

Search engines are interesting things. Without them, the World Wide Web would be an impenetrable morass of data, pictures, videos, music, products, and words. There would be no way for you to find anything. With search engines, the Web is the most incredible information retrieval tool in the history of mankind. And all of this—from the the Defense Advanced Research Projects Agency, visionaries like Ray Tomilson, who invented e-mail, and Tim Berniers-Lee, who invented the World Wide Web, and the others who developed TELNET, File Transfer Protocol (FTP), browsers, and the services that run on the Web to bring us text, graphics, music, and video— depends upon the ability to find and link to it because that is really the power of the Web.

When you send a search request to a search engine, the search engine does not search the entire World Wide Web. It searches its directory, its database, or whatever technology it uses in its data warehouse. It is from the data warehouse that your results come. There is no attempt made to search every server and every Web site in the world to complete your search. That's why when a Web site is submitted to a search engine, it may take weeks before that site actually appears in search results. It takes time for the search engine's spider to visit the site, follow the links it finds there, and bring all that information back to the search engine. That's why we do not recommend using a commercial search engine to find data located on an Intranet. It can be weeks or months before the material shows up in a search. Now lets talk about three major search engines and how to use them well. Why? One of our clients complained that she could not find her site when she searched for it. We easily found it, by simply placing the business name within quotation marks. That was the first problem, but the second and larger problem was that she was using a different search engine than we were. When dealing with clients, just because you can find something does not mean that they can find it, even when that something is the client's own Web site on their favorite search engine. So, here are a few words on how to use Google, Yahoo, and AltaVista well. From what we've seen, the largest problem with users finding material is the user's ability to use a search engine well. We do not say this to insult anyone, but the problem persists because most people just put their search terms into the text box and press search. Keep that in mind, when your client can't find things online. You may find that the problem is in communication rather than anything technical. We recommend telling the client what search engines you will be submitting their site to, determining what search engine he or she uses, and submitting the site there as well. It will make your life so much easier.

As this is written (December 2007), Google has about 50 percent of the Web's search traffic. In August 2007, Google handled 37 billion searches. That's about 1.2 billion searches per day, or about 50 million searches per hour. Google supports a decent range of search characters to help you refine, define, and craft your query. See them here: *www.googleguide.com/ or_operator.html.* You will find:

+ The plus sign. It forces Google to include a term in your search. Do not place a space character between the plus sign and the word. For example: when you wish to include the word, tools, in your search, do so like this: +tools.

- The minus key. When placed in front of a word this causes that word to be ignored in your search. Yankees -baseball will return results that do not contain the Yankees baseball team.

" " Quotation marks. When you wish to search for a phrase, place that phrase in quotation marks. "Planet mars" returns only sites that contain both words. This is an implied Boolean AND search. You can have more than two words in a phrase, of course. And you can search for two strings in the same query, like this: "hand tools" "antique wrenches."

~ The tilde. This searches for the word it precedes, and synonyms as well. When you want a cheap laptop computer, search on ~cheap laptop and you will find that your returns include: inexpensive, affordable, and low cost as well.

OR | The Boolean OR. This searches for one or the other of two terms. Search on cats OR dogs and you will find sites relating to cats or dogs. You will not find sites that relate to cats and dogs. The | character is on your keyboard, look above the \, the back slash key, just above the Enter key. You can issue your search in two ways: cats OR dogs, cats | dogs. The term *Boolean* refers to George Boole, a mathematician who worked out the logic of AND, OR, and other structures.

For even more latitude than what you see here, use Google's Fagan Finder. Google offers Firefox support at *www.faganfinder.com/google2.html*. So, if you use Firefox, give it a minute and it will automatically open that link. If you use Microsoft Explorer, use this link, *www.faganfinder.com/google.html*, and you'll be fine. For Google's Advanced Search, click the Advanced Search link to the right of the text box on Google's main page.

AltaVista has a rich search environment. AltaVista's advanced features are found here, *www.altavista.com/web/adv*. Yahoo includes their advanced features at *www.search.yahoo.com/web/advanced?ei=UTF-8*.

User-Generated and User-Maintained Content

> "There is no fixed rule of this subject of brevity."
>
> —Claude Hopkins

8

Many people and companies develop their own content or maintain their own content. That's fine. This only becomes a problem when they believe that anything is better than nothing and fill the site with fluff. Using fluff is always a mistake. A small amount of high-quality content is far superior to a lot of fluff. Fluff does not fulfill anyone's needs. Except, of course, the person who is paid to write it. When the need for content and the need to keep the cost of content to zero dollars or as low as humanly possible collide, the quality of the content can suffer. "You get what you pay for" is true in the world of Web content, as it is everywhere else. Worse, you can get what you would never pay for—like your Web site may not perform as it should, does not bring in more business, and does not provide resources your customers are looking for. Your Web site is no different from having an employee that does not do his or her job, and needs to exist under the same constraints and criteria that are applied to employees.

When a client takes on the task of writing or updating content, you, as a writer, should not see this as a loss of business, but an opportunity to guide and train the user. While they will have words, sentences, and paragraphs on the site, the material may not do the job of bringing home the bacon. That's where you can help, because the true cost of user-created content can exact a terrible price if that Web site is to be relied upon for economic survival.

Having a user write his own content offers real advantages to the Web master and the customer—initially. But later, having the customer responsible for deriving content can be a serious problem. Why? "Look at the money we saved," says the customer, "and just to write about our business. Wow, what a deal." And the Web master thinks, "Got all that work done at no cost. Cool. Allowed me to quote a very attractive price." Everything is great so far, right? While that seems to be the case, what appears like a good thing all to often becomes a nightmare.

You see, it's like this. Web masters know that they must make a competitive bid to capture the job. No surprise there. So what they do to keep the cost down is not include the cost of the content for the site. Oh sure, they include the development costs, the charges for graphics, hosting, and server setup. You know, all the technical things, because, well hey, they are technical folks. They are not writers and do not want to include money in the bid for doing any writing because other Web masters won't do that. So to keep their cost and their bid low to get the job, content is not included. This is rather like building a house and not planning to put anything in it, but this is literally what is done every day to keep costs low. It's a jungle out there and our Web master needs to survive in that jungle.

So the bid gets written and sent to the client. Either the content will be mentioned in the bid or it won't. What is important is that somewhere along the line our client will be responsible for writing almost all of the words that will be placed on the site. This only looks good *initially*. It's little more than lipstick on a pig. Soon, everyone comes to the realization that the lipstick does not hide the pig. The Web master's client does not make money writing for the Web master. No. The client makes money pushing production out the door. And everyone is about to learn a terrible lesson. While it is fine to save money, making money is what is really truly important, but I am getting ahead of myself.

Our Web master goes to work. There is design to do, then graphics to be chosen and either purchased or made from scratch, a logo to be designed so a graphics artist is brought in, then, maybe, some Flash animation to create, and space on a Web server to be readied. Now, all our Web master need do is add the content that the user wrote and collect the fee. Right? Well, that was the plan. Let's see how it goes in all to many circumstances.

Before we go any further, let me just mention this. Many clients have no Web ability at all. This is hard for many people involved with the Web and technology to understand, but it is true. Many people have real problems even using e-mail. To expect anyone to be able to send text or graphics via e-mail is a bad idea. Any Web master expecting this can have real problems getting data moved across the Net when dealing with a client who is not technically savvy. That is absolutely true and because you are likely a technically savvy person, find it hard to believe. Please believe it. Verify the ability of your clients and gauge what they can do before you expect them to do things that they are not capable of. While your clients will be excellent businesspeople, it does not mean that they can take digital photographs, resize them, and e-mail them to you. No, it does not. It does not mean that they can write and get you content on your schedule either. This is a book on Web content and you are likely thinking that this is exaggerated. It is not an exaggeration. This is reality. Exercise caution whenever you expect your clients to perform outside their area of expertise. Exercise extreme caution. Back to the story.

So our Web guy calls the customer to have the content e-mailed and hears the client say, "I've been really busy and haven't gotten to it. I'll send it next week." Translation: "I've got to get production out the door and that's more important, because I make money from getting production out the door, not writing Web content." Did you notice the word *really*? It is the kiss of death. And the next week when our Web master calls, the customer says, "I've been really busy and haven't gotten to it. I'll send it next week." Sound familiar?

You're a person of the world and know that this is code for "I'm not going to write this, because I have matters that are far more critical to my survival than writing Web content." Hopefully our Web master was smart enough to capture up-front funds to cover the initial costs, because we know of projects that have languished waiting for content. Our Web master is about to learn a terrible lesson. When the needs of pushing production out the door conflict with anything else, getting production out the door wins. Imagine saying to your boss, "I'm not going to do the job you are paying me for, so I can do some writing for the Web guy." Do you think that any employee is going to be given days or weeks to write content? Weeks? You say, "It could not possibly take that long, could it?" Yeah, it could. A novice writer will write and rewrite and rewrite. He or she will use a trillion yellow sticky notes, talk to everyone twice, and make people crazy with constant yearning for validation of what is being written because this is very important. It's important to present the company in a positive light because, well, people will be reading this and on and on and on and on. Giving a non-writer a job of this magnitude is a brutal thing to do and likely this will fall to someone so low on the totem pole that he or she can, literally, not delegate it to someone else.

And what about Search Engine Optimizing the content? Are we to expect that the client's employee who draws the short straw is an expert in researching keywords? Can this person construct adequate title and meta tags? Is our poor sap going to include alt data for graphics? Will the titles of links be adequate or will the links read "Click here"?

The reason we don't like user-generated content has nothing to do with making money. It has everything to do with providing the client with a Web site that will do the job. Giving clients superior customer service is the key to success. Having a client participate in creating a site that can not possibly do the job a client needs it to helps no one.

This shows you what user generated content can cost Web masters and businesses alike. Today, a Web presence is a necessity, it can garner business from around the world or around the corner. Everyone loses when Web projects are delayed. The true cost is anybody's guess.

An example of a poor e-mail

The example shown on page 145 is perhaps the worst e-mail we have ever received from an English-speaking and -writing person. This comes from a business in the Washington, DC, area.

This e-mail violates more than bad writing. It uses a statistic that the reader is free to interpret as the reader sees fit. Never do that. Whenever you cite a statistic, tell the reader why that statistic is important and just what it means in the positive sense to the reader. Never allow the reader to draw his or her own conclusions, because as we've said previously, the conclusion drawn may not be the one you want the reader to draw. This is especially true when the statistic you use is in the vicinity of 50 percent, because it means that half of the sample did what you want and the other half did not do what you want. This can destroy you because it tells the reader that your odds are even that you will or won't like what is being sold. Think about it: How many people would buy something or use something that there was a 50/50 chance that they would not like the product? When using statistics that cut this close, be sure to tell the reader that this is at or better than the industry average. Or use some other words or reassure the reader that the statistic shows far more than what it seems to show. If you can't do that, don't use the statistic. Never allow the reader to draw his or her own conclusions. That's your job.

An E-mail From the Mythical Publishing Company

Here is an example of a poorly written e-mail. It contains a misspelling, is not punctuated, and uses a statistic badly.

> on the program entry form are the rates and we are the oldest and largest publisher of small businesses in the world our sucess rate has always been excellent with over 50% remewals

1. No capitalization of the first word in the sentence.

2. They do not publish "small businesses." They publish information on small businesses.

3. They have a *50% remewals* rate. They mean *renewal* rate.

4. Statistics cut both ways. Never use them without an explanation to guide the reader to the conclusion that you want drawn. Here about half of their clients are lost every year. Is that good? Who knows?

5. The word *sucess* is spelled wrong. The writer means *success*. Misspellings are deadly when you are in business and these people are in the advertising business.

6. No period at the end of the sentence.

Would you want to advertise with people who can't spell, can't punctuate, and admit to losing about half of their business yearly?

Let's rewrite this:

> You will find our rates on the attached Program Entry form. We are the oldest and largest publisher of small business information in the world. Our client renewal rate is in excess of fifty percent, one of the best in the business.

1. Sentences are capitalized.

2. Sentences end with a period.

3. The name of the form is capitalized and the reader is told that it is attached to the e-mail.

4. There are no misspelled words.

5. The statistic leaves nothing to the reader's imagination, stating that this is one of the best retention rates in the business.

Content Management Software

Many of our clients ask to be able to update and maintain their Web sites. This is a smart decision business-wise and can save thousands of dollars in fees to hire a Web master to do the same thing. Only one problem: The client is not technically savvy, else the client would have created the Web site in the beginning. What to do? Well let's see, how about a front end that is simple to use and effective, and allows the client to do their own updates. We just happen to have one to mention, as a matter of fact. This product will pay for itself and the client can have a technically astute person do the updating at little more than the cost of the employee's time, a computer, and an Internet connection. As far as businesses are concerned this is as good as it gets. Who benefits from this the most? Any business that must continually update sales or their venue, like a movie theater. How many times have you looked online to find the time and date of an event only to find sites that are years out of date. Why do you think that all this garbage is left on the Net? No one wants to spend the money to have a geek take it down. Having software that allows users to edit their online world can go a long way to get the garbage out of your searches. That's a good thing. A very good thing.

One of our clients, Laubacher Multimedia, *www.mywebdept.com*, has created a Web content and management product that makes updating and maintaining Web content by nontechnical people possible. To see a live demonstration of this product, visit *www.lmmdevelopment.com/demo.* To see the product and actually use it, go to *www.mywebdept.com/Portal/PortalHome.asp,* and login with: *www.mywebdept.com/ContentManagement.asp.*

Username: guest@mywebdept.com

Password: mywebdept

On the right side of your screen you will see these links; follow them to use the product and actually update material on the *MyWebDept.com* server:

- Web site **management services,** where you add, modify, or remove pages, and *Gallery Manager,* where you manage documents, images and other files like logos.

- My issues, where you can submit a ticket for anything that requires attention. You have the ability to e-mail the ticket to anyone you choose for resolution.

❷ **E-mail marketing** adds people to a list, imports lists, sends lists, and more. You can use this to manage your e-mail marketing campaigns.

❷ **FAQs** will add, edit, or remove your Frequently Asked Questions file(s). FAQs are very popular and users will use them.

❷ **MyBlog** will add a blog and manage entries in your blog. This is a benefit that is not to be underestimated. Having a blog is important to your success, and being able to quickly and easily edit it is a major enhancement to your well being. This will keep you from pulling your hair out.

❷ **MySportsLeague** will update your league, team, and game information.

❷ **Contacts** will set up forms for your Web site. It will take care of the fields, forms, and reporting as well. This is an asset. Forms can be problematic in their coding and can require technical expertise to get them working and designed the way you want them.

Advantages:

❷ You update the content personally. This saves you money and allows you to keep chronological material current and up-to-date quickly and easily.

❷ You update material at your own pace. You do not need to input all of your changes at one time. The product will save the material you are adding or changing on your office computer. When you have completed all of the edits, you can place the material on your Web site for public consumption.

Here is some technical information on the product:

❷ It is a Web-based interface, meaning that you will see, and edit, your Web site as though you are looking it.

❷ Any portion of any Web page can be edited. This includes the replacement of online graphics with graphics from your office computer. This is a real advantage when you work with seasonal or sales material.

❷ Material that is on more than one Web page can be edited once and automatically updated on all pages.

❯ A Versions feature allows you to set and save on your office computer multiple version of a page. This gives you the ability to quickly and easily change your site. All you do is edit any version you like, save it, and upload it. This, too, is excellent for seasonal material because it gives you all the time in the world to get it the way you want it.

❯ Update title tags on your pages. As we've said, title tags are very important to your site being found. The ability to update them is a real asset.

❯ Update keyword and description META tags for your pages.

❯ Add text, pictures, links, and documents to your Web site.

❯ Add tables. Tables are an excellent way to present data.

❯ CSS compliant editor.

❯ HTML view mode allows you to see what your changes look like before you place them online. This is so important that its inclusion cannot be overstated.

If you are not technical, and some of this means little or nothing to you, take heart; we were all there once. This software offers benefits to writers and business owners alike. Why do we say that? Writers lose jobs because the client can't afford the constant cost of updating content. This is true even though the cost of the initial content is acceptable. We have had people actually ask us to train them so that they could get out from under the ongoing cost of updating their sites. With this product, business owners can have the initial writing done by a professional writer and then maintain the material themselves. Writers will appreciate being able to offer clients a way to cost effectively maintain content, while still capturing the initial business and major future updates. So, you see, this product creates a win-win situation for everyone.

9

Communication

"When you once get a person's attention, then is the time to accomplish all you ever hope with him."

—Claude Hopkins

The necessity of communicating to your user, your intended audience, or your reader is paramount for any writer, Web writers included.

Everybody Knows That, Don't They?

We are all affected by the, "Everybody knows that, don't they?" The assumption that other people share your knowledge is a terrible mistake. While the people you deal with every day share your knowledge, do not assume everyone who reads your content does, as well. Everybody does not know what you know. In fact, whenever you find yourself or your clients using the term *they*, take it as a danger sign. What you are doing is painting a group of people or segment of the public with the same brush. Never a good idea. Discuss people, clients, and customers in specific terms. Always write your content so that it makes sense to the user. Never hesitate to spell out precisely and exactly what you want the user to gain, know, or buy.

Red Auerbach said it best: "It's not what you say; it's what they hear." His ability to win games is proof positive that he knew the secret of communication. He spoke to his players in terms that the players understood. This can be recast for writers as: It's not what you write; it's what they read. There's a message there.

You must, absolutely must, write to the user's level of understanding, education, wants, needs, and desires. Do not write for the sales staff, engineers, or yourself. Write for the user.

Communication—Just What Is That?

Communication takes place (or doesn't) between people, and for any communication to be successful, three things are needed: a common language, a common grammar, and common knowledge of the definition of words used. Here are a couple of examples of what can happen when those things are not met. The former prime minister of Australia, when answering a question in Japan, said, "I am not here to play funny buggers"; meaning he was not about to split hairs. This was translated as "I am not here to play laughing homosexuals." Another Australian diplomat tried to tell his French audience that his career, as he looked back on it, was divided into two parts: boredom before he came to Paris, and excitement now. Instead he said, "When I look at my backside, I find it is divided into two parts." (Both examples are from *The Week*, "Lost in translation"; September 14, 2007.)

These are fine examples of communications that did not function as intended. This must not happen with your words. Should words and your audience not fulfill the three criteria, you need to do something about it.

A knowledge of grammar is critical in written and verbal communications, because so much of what people say gets written down. English is a complex language with a complex grammar. You can count on your reader knowing that a sentence begins with an uppercase letter, that the words will be separated with spaces, and that a period (.), question mark (?), or exclamation point (!) will end the sentence. These are arguably the three most important and best-known facts in the English language. Without knowing them, written material is nothing but gibberish.

Communication is not about telling, talking, or writing; it is about understanding. When you write for the Web, for print, or for a business card, brochure, or book you do not have the luxury of knowing your readers personally. So, construct your content for the intended reader. That is imperative and so critically important that it can not be overstated. If your reader is a teenager and you are writing an explanation of a product, take into account that parents and grandparents will be reading this material when shopping for a gift.

On the Web, your competition is only a click away. People will open multiple sites, each in its own window, and compare goods and services head to head. Sure, price counts. So does the cost of shipping, but how you explain and present the product counts as well. It counts a very great deal, because when you write to appear more knowledgeable and have better description, people will do business with you because those details increase your credibility.

Also, keep in mind the goods. Are you writing about a luxury automobile? You need to write to a well-to-do adult and show why this car enhances his or her appearance, authority, prestige, and sex appeal. People buy expensive things to show the world that they can afford them. Think of an expensive sports car driven by a young professional as a piece of jewelry and you won't go wrong. If you're writing to sell a Hummer, you will write differently than for a sports car because a Hummer is a big, bad, go-anywhere vehicle for people with gas money to burn. Write to that mindset. Write to that need to fulfill that want. Be sure your description satisfies the need(s) of the user. Ask yourself who buys this product. Research, and only research, will tell you the answer. If you doubt that, talk to any copywriter who writes advertising. These people spend weeks doing research and talking to owners, the manufacturer, employees, and sales staff. They do their homework and so should you.

Show, Don't Tell

When you spend time with writers, you will hear them talking about showing versus telling. What they means is this: Don't tell the reader; show the reader with a "word picture." Actually make a word picture, a story, of what it is that you are trying to convey. Here is an example how you might want to convey that the day was "just gorgeous and you enjoyed being outside tremendously":

Tell: It was a beautiful day.

Show: As the golden sun rose over the horizon, there was not a cloud in the sky. The clear, intense sunlight painted the fall foliage a riot of red, orange, yellow, and green. The sparkling air held a crisp, clean chill. It made you glad to be alive.

What a difference! Show your users; don't tell them. Convey information with a story and make the reader an active part of it, with a rich and interesting word picture. Note: We say a chill in the air because it is appropriate to the season. Keep your picture interesting and appropriate. When skiing, things are cold. At the beach, you expect to be warm or hot. Make it real. If it's appropriate, it will be real.

Showing rather than telling is important to the success of your content. Making your words entertaining and interesting to read will go a long way to getting them read. And that is the point of everything that gets placed on the Net. No one puts material on the Net in hope that it will not be read. Write in an entertaining manner whether you are doing an advertisement, a product description, or a software documentation. Even an ad on eBay can be well written, interesting to read, and still effective. In fact, any ad that is well written and interesting will be far more effective than the competition that is not. So, if you want your words to move product, make your words relate to the customer and do so in an entertaining engaging manner. Online your competition is only a click away.

Experience Widely and Read Widely

The more experience you gain and the reading you do, the better. While you may never gain firsthand experience, you can read the accounts of others. Read about what you like and what you don't like. Go to museums to view paintings and sculpture. Talk to people about everything, from politics to the future of the Web. Gain as wide an experience base as you possibly can. It will be an incredible asset to you, making your writing rich, vibrant, and alive— a pleasure to read.

Write outside your immediate sphere of interest and do the necessary research to make it come alive. Write a short story, publish something on the Web, or write for a newsletter, magazine, tabloid, or newspaper. Create an e-book, write a press release, volunteer to teach something, or teach someone to read. Take a part-time job, or several, for the experiences they offer. Join a club, or start a writer's group. Ride with your local police or volunteer at a local television station. These things require little in the way of out-of-pocket expenses and will round you out nicely. Carry a small notebook and jot down interesting names, addresses, books, and snippets of conversation. That is how many writers create terrific dialogue; they make notes of actual conversations. Nothing is better than the real thing.

Advertisers have done this for ages and spend time in the factories of their clients, with installers, salespeople, and the buyers as well. This allows them to gain a wide experience and knowledge base necessary to the production of high-end sales literature and Web content. You can do that as well. Beyond this, network weekly or a couple times per month at least. There are many organizations out there. Call your chamber of commerce to get started. The more you rub shoulders with businesspeople and the general public the stronger your prose will be. After all, you are writing for them. It only makes sense to know how they see the world, the words they use, what is important, and how they get their news and information. Once you know this, read, listen to, or view those sources so you know what your target audience knows.

This kind of knowledge of your target audience is invaluable to your work and your future. The more effective your words, the easier it is for you to attract more work. Imagine that, and all from getting out of the office. When Sam Walton was developing WalMart, he spent one-half day per week in the office and he said that he was trying to cut that down. He knew the value of knowing what was going on with the people who were important to him. He went so far as to bring coffee and donuts to the men and women who worked on loading docks. Knowing what works and what does not work is absolutely critical to success. Sam knew that. Now you do, too. Find out what your readers know and what they need to know, and then tell them in words and sentences that speak their language. Not your language, their language.

Who Are Users?

The term *users* refers to the people who use the Web. Originally, before the Web existed, it referred to the people who used the programs and products that software vendors produced. Today, we use the term to refer to the people who surf the Web and read our material. Welcome to the Web; you now have users.

Some people do not like to use the word *users* because it sounds strange or condescending. Some people just plain don't like it and that is understandable, as no one likes to be used. However, that is not the intent of the word. You are not trying to manipulate or use anyone. It is simply a term that refers to the people who use your product. In this case the product is the Web site for which you are writing or that you are developing. When meeting with clients it is a good idea to tell them that when you use the word *user*, you are referring to the people who will be reading their Web site. Better yet, refer to them as readers to remove all doubt. This way the client knows who you are referring to and that you mean no disrespect. That is always a good thing because, should your client take a dislike to you for any reason, he or she will never like your work.

How users read the Web

Users do not read the Web in the same way that they read printed matter. The kiss of death to any Web site is large blocks of text. No one is going to read all that. So, don't write it.

» Users will not read your text thoroughly, in a word-by-word manner similar to reading a book.

» The first two paragraphs of a section are key and need to state the important information that follows.

» Your subheads and bullets need to contain information-carrying words.

» The opening sentence of a paragraph needs to inform the user of what the paragraph contains.

» Headings must be informative of what follows.

» Links need to be accurate and informative so that users can decide if the information they seek follows the link. Poorly named links just don't work, nor do deceptive links.

Research from Jakob Nielsen

Here is a research project and its findings from Jakob Nielsen, entitled "F-Shaped Pattern For Reading Web Content." See: *www.useit.com/alertbox/reading_pattern.html.* This study shows that users usually read the Web in two horizontal passes and one vertical pass as measured in eye movement studies. For us, this shows conclusively that users do not read the Web as they read a book, magazine, or newspaper. Use this knowledge to your benefit when you construct your content, by being sure that your headings and subheadings introduce the most important material first. This is similar to the inverted pyramid style of writing. Users want the information they are looking for to be obvious, and listed under heads and subheads that make sense.

Technical Versus Nontechnical Users

Technical users make lousy testers. They can make anything work. When you are testing your site, be sure to include both technically savvy people and those who represent the level of ability that you expect from the general public or those who will be using your site on a daily basis. Pay close attention to the challenges nontechnical people are having with your site. Remember that most of the general public fall into the less skilled category.

A programmer friend of ours once tested a program he had written by having our secretary run the code. She had been in the group for years and knew the job and was a skilled user. The programmer's first input asked for the date. Sounds simple enough, doesn't it? The only problem is, once you code a program for the date, that is the only format that the program will take. Our programmer friend programmed the date to be input like this: dd/mm/yy, (dayday/monthmonth/yearyear): 02/12/07. Sounds simple enough? It wasn't. The secretary entered: 2 February 2007 and the program crashed. No surprise there. You see what happened? The programmer made an assumption. He assumed that the user would enter the date in the same format that he used, and did not tell the user what that format was. This type of thing can be an annoyance or terribly expensive. NASA lost a Mars space craft because a portion of the work was done in England and, when it was returned to the United States, the readouts did not list any units. NASA assumed metric units and the makers used English units. Not the same at all. The result? Lost mission. See *www.cnn.com/TECH/space/9909/30/mars.metric.02/* or Google "nasa lost mars mission."

There are consequences to not telling people what you are doing, in terms that they can understand. Communication is about forming a message in the mind of your user, reader, listener, or viewer that matches what you want the message to be. The consequences for poor communications go from humorous, to inexpensive, to expensive, to deadly. Appendix E contains a short section on "should and shall." The misuse of these two words can cost thousands, maybe tens of thousands, of dollars to straighten out. They are not the same. They are not interchangeable. When you take the responsibility for writing content do so thoroughly and competently in words that your intended reader finds meaningful. Or, do everyone a favor, and pass the job, subcontract it if you must, to someone who will.

Gain Users' Trust

Credibility is important on the Web. The quality of content does affect users perceptions of the trustworthiness of the material. Is your site well done? A tasteful Web site will enhance your credibility, as will the quality of your outbound links, because they allow the user to determine if what you are saying is true.

This is not the place for vulgarity. Never seek to use language that users may find objectionable. Write for conservative readers, else your content will not be read by them and you will push away a segment of the population.

Here is a case of a deceptivly titled link involving Web site where users rent movies. At check out, users are told that if they follow a particular link they will receive a free movie for being such a good customer. What is there, somewhere, but certainly not made obvious, is the fact that when the users follow the free movie link, they will have their credit card number forwarded to a Web site that begins billing them for $9.95 per month. This is deceptive, criminal behavior, and no way to treat people. This destroyed trust in everyone concerned and only drives home the fact that people on the Net can't be trusted. Do not run the risk of losing people's trust. You will never regain it. In the previous example, those companies who used this service to send their customers into an unknown, unwanted monthly charge behaved criminally.

We've shown you deceptive tactics. More realistic is a fact or statement that is wrong or nearly right, but not quite. Fact checking is important and not to be underestimated. There are several things you can do. Print out the material and have it read and verified. When you are working, maintain a list of your research and where the data came from. Best of all, have the data independently verified by a third party. When you are building your research database, use a spreadsheet to record the Web site address or other source of the material. When taking information from the Web, consider copying the Web site to your hard drive. Using data from a site no longer on the Web is problematic at best. At least with the information on your hard drive, you can show that it did indeed exist. Or you can upload the no-longer-on-the-Web material to your site and so mirror the material where it can be accessed by anyone.

If a product is trademarked, be kind enough to include the ™ symbol. This is often overlooked. Verify the spelling of all names, titles, telephone and fax numbers, and e-mail addresses. Do not rely on secondary sources. Just because a Web site references an article in a newspaper or magazine does not mean that the article exists or ever existed there. Go to the original source and verify it. There are few times in life where one can say never or always. This is one of those times. Never expose yourself to being unable to cite the source of your facts. Always create a paper trail to protect yourself. When dealing with money, verify that the currency symbol is correct. This is especially important when dealing with money transfer data or money conversion data, where it is critical to know how many dollars, let's say, relate to their equivalent in euros or yen. As not all word processors have these symbols, you may need to obtain a font that does, spell out the word, or obtain the symbol online.

$ The United States dollar, of course, and ¢ is the symbol for United States cents.

£   The British Pound Sterling, the currency of England, Scotland, and the United Kingdom's territories.

¥   The yen, the standard monetary unit of Japan.

RMB   China's Renminbi.

€   The euro, the exclusive currency of Austria, Belgium, Finland, France (except Pacific territories using the CFP franc), Germany, Greece, Ireland, Italy, Luxembourg, The Netherlands, Portugal, and Spain.

What Users Want

➡ Information quickly.

➡ A consistent look to your Web site. They want to see that your navigational links are the same from page to page.

➡ To easily be able to return to your home page.

➡ Links that take them where the links say they will take them.

➡ Working links.

➡ Clear, unambiguous writing that is easily understood.

➡ Short paragraphs with an informative opening sentence.

➡ Text that is short or broken up.

➡ Text targeted and to the point. Do not wander. Write tight.

What Users Do Not Want

There are things that users most definitely do not want, and these are things that you most definitely want to take pains to be sure that your site does not contain, because once users have decided that they do not like your site you won't see them again.

- Users do not like to wait.

- Users get bored quickly. Waiting for pictures bores users just as fast as waiting for text.

- They do not want to have to slog though large amounts of text looking for one key nugget of information.

- They do not want to become lost at your Web site.

- They do not want pages that say "Under Construction." When the page is ready, put it up on the Web.

- Users do not like pages that scroll and scroll and scroll forever. Keep pages short.

- Users hate anything resembling marketing fluff. They prefer factual information. So, do not mix marketing and sales materials in the same paragraph or block of text that contains factual information. Marketing is fine, but not there.

Conclusion: Why Words Matter

Can you think of something that you don't have a word for? This is difficult, perhaps not even possible, because with no word to describe it there is no substance, no definition, no description of the item.

Words matter.

How you describe events, things, people, processes—it all matters. When there is not a word, you may have to make one. Consider laser. It is an acronym for Light Amplification and Stimulated Emission of Radiation (LASER). Without a word to define it, what would you call it? Words give us a reference to the mental grouping that the word, and the thing, fall into. Think of electronic mail, which became known as e-mail. Notice how the word is recognizable because it attaches itself to the concept of mail, a centuries-old word and concept. E-mail was not called the electronic pony express, or the electronic and computer-generated multilingual information transport system. Electronic mail is almost instantly recognizable. You likely use a local area network (LAN) when you send messages from computer to computer. This is not called mail because it's a message that appears onscreen. You can't save it or print it. All you can do is read it.

While estimates vary, educated people use about 35,000 words in their lifetimes. This is a measure of the range of thought that the person is capable of thinking and the range of perceptions that the person becomes capable of taking in. When you are writing to motivate people to give money to a charity, you want to remember that. In fact, remembering that is a good idea no matter what you write. If your words are outside the active vocabulary of the intended reader, you are wasting your time. When something is outside the normal range it is either not noticed, noticed but ignored, or noticed and then quickly forgotten.

Here is an example that uses photography instead of words. Have you ever seen pictures of beautiful people in advertising or on calendars? While the pretty people do grab attention, that attention is quickly lost. Words are like that. If outside of your reference system, they just can't make an impact. Use words within the reference system of your intended reader. How do you find those words? Find where your intended reader is and go there. Listen to conversations; read what they read; talk to them. That is precisely what advertising people do. They do this to learn the industry and the product, and in the process they gain the words and definitions surrounding the product. Their cognition increases and they are then able to express themselves in words that are meaningful to the intended reader, because they have insight into the words that the intended reader uses to conceptualize the product, service, or item in question. Want proof? Find a copy of any magazine that runs small advertisements in the back of the magazine. Now go back over the months and years. Some of these ads have not changed in ages. Why is that? It's because they are effective. They work, and the writer knows that, because other words have been tested and found not to work as well. When you find good words, stay with them. Don't change a winner without good reason. If you must experiment, or need to upgrade your material, test the new material and see how it performs. And then decide, from a position of knowledge and strength.

Podcasting

"Don't say the old lady screamed. Bring her on and let her scream."

—Mark Twain

10

You can be the king, or queen, of the small sound stage or screen. What is a podcast? It is audio or video content that you place on a Web site where it can be downloaded onto an iPod, or similar device, for viewing or listening at a later time.

A podcast is a moving pictures expert group, MPEG, file. Actually, an MP3 file. So, when you create your podcast, you will either create it as an MPEG or convert it to an MP3 file from whatever format in which you created it. When you create the podcast, follow what we present in the training section on page 76. Please do not go off willy-nilly and just start talking about something that you love or know a lot about. No one wants to hear you ramble on and on. Always provide structure to your material. Your podcast must have a beginning, a middle, and an end. This presupposes structure. It does not presuppose an unorganized, unstructured rambling account that will be of no interest to anyone. To ramble is the kiss of death.

Podcasting allows you to actually show your users how you do things and can be used for training, product advertising, entertainment, and just plain having fun. A podcast is perfect for instructions on how to use computer software, job-related tasks, for operating complex devices, and other things that would benefit from being able to place audio or video instructions literally in someone's pocket. Who knows? You may be able to turn this feature into a lucrative source of additional income. Some people do believe that podcasting will be even bigger than blogging. Actually, we share that opinion. Time will tell.

To record an audio podcast, we recommend Audacity, which you can download for free at *www.audacity.sourceforge.net*. You will also need to obtain the LAME library to export your recorded audio file to MP3. You will find LAME at *www.lame.sourceforge.net/index.php*. You will need the LAME library because Audacity saves its recordings in .aup format, which many other programs cannot open or deal with. So, to export to MP3, you need LAME.

Creating a Podcast

Creating a podcast is easy. You will need: Audacity, a microphone, LAME, and some time. Plug in your microphone, configure Audacity to record from the mike, begin recording, and start talking. Save your file and export it to MP3, then upload the MP3 to a server and link to it, and there you are. Your podcast is alive and well on your site. Simple? Yes it was, but, like all things simple, there is more to the story. When you are finished saving and exporting your MP3, be sure to close the window or begin a new project to avoid laying another track on top of your previous work. Of course, you will need a quiet place to make the recording so that traffic, airplanes, and other background noise will not find their way into your recording.

Working With Guests or Talent

When you interview guests, preplanning is the word, and the way to a hassle-free experience for everyone and to an excellent podcast for you. Your preparation consists of two things. First, being sure that your hardware and software are in perfect operating condition. This includes seeing to it that any battery powered equipment has fresh, or fully charged batteries. Here is an old trick. Do a "dry run" and practice. Record yourself and adjust all your hardware and software so that everything is ready to go when your guests arrive. This avoids having technical problems when the guests are in the studio. Do the preplanning and verify that everything is ready to go before your guests arrive. In addition to the technical details you want to be sure that you have comfortable chairs for everyone, a table, and enough room for people to stand, walk around, and sit comfortably. If you are going to offer coffee or other refreshments, be sure that they arrive in plenty of time so you don't need to run out to get them.

Be sure you have enough microphones for all your guests, or a single microphone that is capable of recording everyone's voice from a central location. You do not want to have to contact people and schedule another session because of technical problems. In fact, should you be interviewing politicians or other professionals, this may not be an option. Also, technical incompetence of this magnitude will peg you as an amateur and you definitely do not want that.

Okay, so much for hardware and software. Second, we come to your home-work. Be sure to write down a list of talking points; don't trust your memory. It is a good idea to have more material than you can cover in the allotted time so that, should the interview move faster than you anticipated, you will not run out of material. Be sure to know the position of your guest(s) on every major point you will be discussing, and be sure that your guests know ahead of time what will be discussed and stick to the plan. Do not, under any circumstances, lure people to your studio and then conduct an ambush interview. Further, knowing the position of your guests on an issue will allow you to put together guests with opposing or differing views. This will make for a much more lively interview. Nothing is worse than listening to a group of people in complete agreement.

If you are doing your podcast professionally to explain a product, training, or advertising, you will likely want to work with experienced people—what we call talent. Using friends and others who have no media experience is a bad idea. So where do you get experienced people?

» A college or university drama club

» Your local community theater group

» Community television

» Community radio

These places can provide you with experienced people willing to work with you. Before you actually make the recording, speak to a lawyer and be sure that your rights are protected. At a minimum, you want a signed document that gives you the right to use the voice of your talent professionally. Get the permission form signed before you make the recording. This means no signed statement, no recording session. When you are interviewing these people, tell them that they are expected to sign your permission slip before the recording session begins. Be sure to get the person's full name, address, town, state, zip code, phone number, and e-mail address. Should you need to contact this person again, you must have the necessary information to do so. Include a contract or letter of agreement that stipulates what they will be paid and what they are expected to do. Be careful of using a time-limited agreement for your recording session. Once you commit to letting everyone go at, let's say, 4 p.m., they are entitled to leave at that time and receive full pay as well. Should your recording session run longer than you expect, this could be trouble.

When working with minors, whether young children or teenagers, you must have written and signed permission of the legal guardian or parent. There are also child protection laws that govern how long a child can work. It is in your best interest to be aware of those laws.

One last note on your financial protection. When dealing with the public in any sort of professional capacity, you need to take into account the need to protect your personal assets in the event that you are sued. We recommend a statement in your contract to the effect that liability is the amount of the contract only. For the specific legal words and phrasing speak to your lawyer. Forming a Limited Liability Corporation (LLC), or other appropriate business entity, is not difficult or expensive. If you are a starving college kid, this is of less importance, but if you own your own home and have a family and assets, you should take steps to protect those assets. Having a corporate structure may be a very good idea for you. Certainly speak to your accountant or a lawyer about this, if you have any doubt. Even something like an automobile accident while you are on company business could pose problems if you get sued. Forming a corporation puts only your corporate assets at risk. For these reasons, we suggest you protect your personal assets with a corporate structure. Better that than losing a home or a life's work.

Sound Recording Equipment

There is a great deal of equipment out there that will provide for your needs. This list is not exhaustive, but it will give you an idea of what is needed and what decent sound recording equipment will cost you. Of course, if you are just getting started, you won't want to invest the $500 or so that is listed here. Still, when you need equipment this will give you a ballpark idea of what things to look for.

- A 1GB flash recording device with line-in, for recording from any audio source. Cost: about $150.

- A high-quality microphone. A large diaphragm condenser microphone suitable for professional vocals. Cost: $175

- A microphone pre amplifier with phantom power. Cost: $70.

- A desktop boom stand for the microphone. Cost: $40.

- A 5-foot microphone cable. Cost: $20.

- A pop filter to clean up the audio signal. Cost: $30.

- Closed headphones to prevent your source audio from being recorded by the microphone. Costs vary widely, but you need spend no more than $40.

Sound Recording Software

With all that hardware you will need some software to get your sweet voice into your computer and to edit and save it later.

Skype

If you will be recording telephone conversations you can use Skype, *www.skype.com*. It is very powerful and will do a great job. Skype is literally free online telephony. Skype offers various ways to record conversations and can use downloadable, additional programs to monitor sound levels and volume as they are recorded on your computer.

Audacity

Audacity is compatible with Windows, Mac, and Linux. It is a free download, and a powerful and useful program. Created by volunteers who wanted to give something back to the Internet, it shows what can be done by people who are highly intelligent, are highly motivated, and want to make a product that will run on major platforms.

- Records live audio via microphone(s) or mixer channels.

- Up to 16 channels simultaneously.

- Imports various sound formats for editing or mixing.

- Exports your final project to WAV, AIFF, AU, and MP3.

- Offers an unlimited number of Undo and Redo commands.

- Can create an unlimited number of audio tracks.

- Removes static, hiss, hum, and other constant background noise.

- Effects offered include: Echo, Phaser, Wahwah, Reverse. These effects can be expanded by incorporating third-party plug-ins.

- Records audio quality of up to 96 kHz.

- Audacity can digitize analog audio from cassette tape and vinyl records. This feature is found in many commercial products. Audacity is a fantastic product available via free download.

Garageband for your Mac

Garageband makes creating royalty free music easy to do with hundreds of music loops. Many loops can be edited to create the mood you want for the podcast. And, let's face it: The attraction of music that is free of the cost of royalties is a serious attraction. Garageband will:

- Handle eight tracks at the same time with its multitrack feature.

- Provide you a real time display of your music with notation.

- Allow you to change the tempo and key of your user recorded instruments during the editing process at any time.

- Save your recordings as loops.

What Graggeband will not do is allow you to apply dynamic audio effects beyond 30 minutes or 999 on its counter.

Adding Music to Your Podcast

Having music on a podcast can go a long way to set a mood and provide a pleasing background ambiance. You can get music at many places on the Web. Music created by other people is not necessarily free for you to use without purchasing royalties. Here are a couple of links to Web sites where you can license music for podcasts and other uses as well.

- Freeplaymusic.com

  - Terms of use, *www.freeplaymusic.com/licensing/termsofuse.php*

  - Rates, *www.freeplaymusic.com/licensing/ratecard.php*

➠ Harryfox.com

❯ Chris Boyd, singer/songwriter/guitarist for Rhode Island's "Big Red and the Resonators" and a dear friend, recommended Harry Fox, *www.harryfox.com*, as a source of professional music licensing. HFA represents music publishers for licensing for CDs and digital downloads, and the Web site include the a Songfile licensing tool, definitions of musical terms, and more.

Parts of a Podcast

1. The Introduction

The first words on your podcast leave an impression and set the tone for all that follows. They can help establish you as someone that your users want to follow and listen to, and someone whose work will be looked for. The words you choose in your introduction can also hinder those goals. Always strive for a consistent introduction that is uniquely yours to add that professional touch.

2. Theme Music

Just as you can recognize a particular song from a movie, you want your podcasts to be identified by a particular song that you have permission to use or one that you create. Either way, to brand your work with a song will tie your podcasts to that song and make people think of you when they hear it. Don't forget you can use different music for the opening and closing.

3. The Greeting

Whatever you initially decide to use for your greeting, continue using it permanently. You want your podcasts to have a consistent opening. Here, too, think of the movies. Who hasn't seen and heard the MGM lion roar at the beginning of one of their movies? Consistency is key. What to include?

❯ The name of the podcast or show.

❯ The name of the host and those interviewed or who is appearing as a guest.

❯ The location, if appropriate, or simply, "From the studios of...."

❯ Your exit; always strive to leave your audience wanting more. Write a closing that tells what you do and what the listener can look forward to in your other podcasts. They have stayed with you to the end and you should expect that they will want to find more of your work. Make it easy for your listeners to see what else you have available.

❯ Create a catchphrase, a few words that define your product, and use that phrase when you are ending your podcast. Create a unique phrase that is easy to remember and your customers will associate it with you and your work.

❯ Credits.

❯ Include your name.

❯ List Web sites where past shows can be found.

❯ Don't forget to include special thanks to those who endorse or support your work. Thanking people goes a long way to maintain relationships.

Software to Upload Your Podcast

When you have a podcast you will need to move it to the server that will place it online. File Transfer Protocol is the software you will use to do that. There are many online to choose from. Here are some, all of which we have used.

CuteFTP, *www.cuteftp.com*, is a product that you must purchase after 30 days, but can download a trial version for free. It is our favorite FTP product. We have used one or another version of this fine software for a lot of years. It's good stuff. We like the professional edition.

SmartFTP, *www.smartftp.com*, is another favorite. You may download a trial version free.

FileZilla, *www.filezilla-project.org*, is free opensource software.

Fire-FTP, *www.fireftp.mozdev.org*, is a free add-on for the Firefox browser. A solid product that does not have the bells and whistles of cuteFTP and SmartFTP, nevertheless it will do the job.

Notifying the World of Your New Podcast

Now that your podcast is complete and online you will want everyone everywhere to know about it. To notify podcast servers of your new work, you will use Ping, a program that sends a signal to the server you wish to notify that says, "Hey, look at me. I've got something new to tell you about."

This gets the server's attention and, hopefully, the server will send a robot to investigate, read the words associated with the new podcast, and bring back the data for search engines to find. You can use Ping either automatically from some of the software you will be using or manually. To do a manual ping, go to the site that you want to ping and find the page that they offer you, to ping them. Follow the instructions and you're home free.

To open a Command window on a Windows computer: Start, Run, CMD, then enter Ping and press the Enter key.

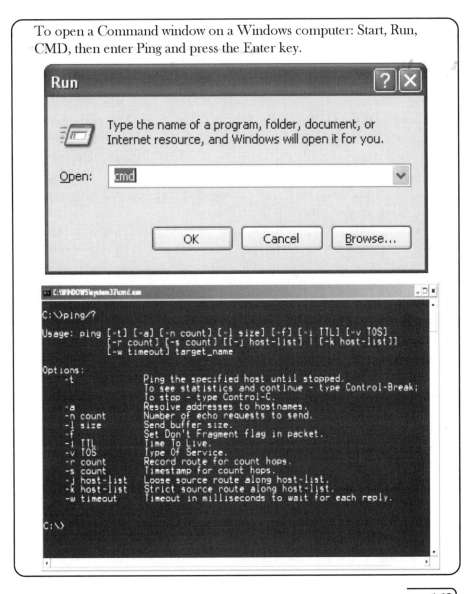

Technical Stuff

File naming

There are several things to consider when you name your podcast files. We suggest you think about this and develop a naming convention that avoids randomness and a bunch of MP3 files in your online directory and on your development computer. Do this before you start making podcasts so that your naming scheme identifies the content of the podcast and the date it was created.

On your Windows computer, upper and lowercase characters are treated alike. This may not be the case on your server. A file named PodCast.mp3 may or may not be able to be accessed by calling for podcast.mp3. Keep that in mind. When you name your files do so in a manner that you will follow religiously forever. Let's say you have a podcast on Web tips created on February 1, 2009. A good name would be, WebTips01-02012009. Should you wish to publish numerous files on Web tips, name them like this: WebTips02-02012009, WebTips03-02152009, WebTips03-02252009, and so on. The 01 following WebTips ensures that your files will sort from 01 to 99 on your development computer and on your server. That is why the leading zero is included. Whatever naming convention you choose, you want to stay with it because when you link to a podcast file the characters in the link must match the characters in the file name precisely. The name of the file and the link must be identical.

File compression

In the online world, less is more; hence the need for file compression and placing files online that are no larger than they need to be. It is in everyone's best interest to create files that are as small as possible while being able to adequately accomplish their mission. Podcasting is no exception to that. Do this by choosing a bit rate that is adequate for the needs of the podcast. This will vary as podcasts vary. There is no reason to make the bit rate greater than what is required for acceptable performance. In fact, doing that only causes increased download time and additional overhead for the net.

Search engine ranking

Ah, search engines, here we go again. Getting your podcast found is dependent on the text that is associated with it. No surprise there. Take a look at your show notes and boil them down to the essence of what your podcast is about. Make a list of the most important words and phrases that capture the subject matter of the podcast. Now, include these words or phrases in the title of the podcast. When people search for podcasts like yours, they will use these words and phrases and when they do, hopefully they will find your podcast. Do not use cute titles or intentionally misspelled words because you like them. This will make your podcast impossible for users to find. What is an intentionally misspelled word? Spelling tunes as tunz. While cute, it will consign your podcast to obscurity forever. How about tortoise? Spell it tortus and it will never be found by anyone but you.

Bit rate

The bit rate is how many bits are being transferred between two points per second and is usually measured in thousands of bits per second or kilo-bits per second, Kbps. The higher the bit rate, the larger your file size will need to be and the better the quality of your podcast. The trick, of course, is to get the best quality podcast for the file size created. Do this by experimenting. If your podcast will only contain your voice, begin at the lowest bit rate. If you need to include music, you will want better quality and a higher bit rate. If you want CD-quality sound, that is one thing. If you want an acceptable background song, that is something else. Match the needs of the music to the needs of the podcast.

You can change the bit rate in Audacity or iTunes. Compress your podcast using one bit rate and save it. Then change the bit rate and save it again with a similar but different name. For example, you can name your first file test.mp3 and the second test1.mp3, for purposes of quality determination only. Now listen to both files and choose the one that gives the best sound quality. When satisfied that you have acceptable quality, there is no need to choose a higher bit rate. Your goal is acceptable quality at the lowest possible bit rate, and hence the smallest file size.

When you have determined which file best serves your needs, rename it to conform to your podcast naming convention and upload it. And, oh yes, delete the test file(s) that you no longer need. Having junk on your development computer is a dangerous thing to do. These files can cause you real headaches if they get where they shouldn't or get used for things that they are not intended for. Get rid of your development files when you no longer need them.

Here are some bit rates:

» 8 Kbps is the quality or a telephone conversation.

» 32 Kbps is the quality of AM radio.

» 96 Kbps is the quality of FM radio.

» 128 Kbps is the quality of a CD and used for MP3 compressed music.

» 1411 Kbps maximum quality of CD audio, with stereo playback capability, 16 bit audio.

Sampling rate

This is a measure of audio samples taken from a continuous signal. The more you sample your audio, the closer you get to representing the actual quality of the audio. Here are some sample rates and their associated technology:

» 8,000 Hz (8 kHz) is telephone quality or lo-fi.

» 22,050 Hz (22 kHz) is equal to AM radio transmission.

» 32,000 (32 kHx) is equal to FM radio transmission and the minimum quality of a miniDV digital recorder.

» 44,100 (44 kHz) is audio CD quality.

» 48,000 (48 kHz) is digital TV, DVD films, and maximum quality on miniDV video camcorder, and professional-grade audio recording.

» Sampling rates can be changed in Audacity and iTunes.

Sampling and bit rate can be confusing and, while you may never need to appreciate the difference, a few more sentences can't hurt. Think of making, well, anything really. Let's say pudding. The more you sample the pudding you send to customers, the more sure you are that they are getting the best possible quality. In audio, the same holds true. The more you sample, the more your samples represent the reality of your product.

ID3 tags

These tags can contain the name or the podcast, artist or creator, album name (if any), track number, year created, composer (if music), genre, and comments. This information allows you to definitively set your podcast apart from all others. You can create and edit your ID3 tags in Audacity and iTunes.

Creating a Video Podcast

A video podcast may be called a vidcast or vodcast. Either way it is an audio/video file uploaded to the Web for download by friends, colleagues, customers, and clients. In this, it is similar to an audio podcast and much of what is previously mentioned will hold true whether you are making video or audio podcasts. Obviously, you will need a video camera and a cable to connect to your computer or other technology to move the unedited video file(s) into your computer for editing. Save the edited video and export it. Be sure to select a resolution of 320 by 240 pixels. Yes, it is small, but you are recording for an iPod, after all.

With a readily available over-the-counter digital camcorder, and some editing software, you can turn out fine video podcast. Here, too, we caution you to not ramble in your audio and in the images you shoot. Use our training checklist, if you have to. Staying on track and on message is vital when working with talent, either professional talent or people who were "volunteered" for the job. Having your material pre-scripted is the way to go. Being able to give direction before the podcast is made is an invaluable asset to turning out a quality product. When you are actually recording your podcast, shoot plenty of video. Don't hesitate to do as many retakes as you feel are needed. What you want is lots of video "in the can" so that you do not have to do a reshoot later. Doing a reshoot is expensive and time-consuming, and you may not be able to get everyone back at the same time easily. Having a great deal of video recording material means that later when you edit you have the material needed to complete your work in the studio. Hence, our advice is to shoot a great deal of material. To do so, make sure you have much more blank recording media than you can possibly use and plenty of fully charged batteries.

You can then place your video podcast as an enclosure on a blogging service. To publish a podcast using a Really Simple Syndication (RSS) feed, you will need to use a Web server, like FeedBurner, *www.feedburner.com*, that can handle this sort of thing. Any RSS feed provider will make it easy to create an RSS file from your blog. You can then reach an audience of millions, literally millions, of people. You will need to provide the link to the podcast RSS feed, and all episodes within the podcast must be available as .m4v, .mp4, or .mov video file enclosures. An iPod can play the following formats:

❯ H.264 video, up to 1.5 Mbps, 640 by 480 pixels, 30 frames per second, Low-Complexity version of the H.264 Baseline Profile with AAC-LC audio up to 160 Kbps, 48 kHz, stereo audio in .m4v, .mp4, and .mov file formats.

❯ H.264 video, up to 768 Kbps, 320 by 240 pixels, 30 frames per second, Baseline Profile up to Level 1.3 with AAC-LC audio up to 160 Kbps, 48 kHz, stereo audio in .m4v, .mp4, and .mov file formats.

❯ MPEG-4 video, up to 2.5 Mbps, 640 by 480 pixels, 30 frames per second, Simple Profile with AAC-LC audio up to 160 Kbps, 48 kHz, stereo audio in .m4v, .mp4, and .mov file formats.

Should you want to place information that is on your screen into a video podcast, we recommend Snagit, *www.techsmith.com/screen-capture.asp*, screen capture software. Snagit will record a video of your screen activity very nicely and is free to use for 30 days; after that, you must purchase it. SnagIt8 creates an AVI file, which must be converted to an MP3. There are plenty of programs on the net to do this.

So, there you are; while this is not an exhaustive section on all things podcast-related, it should be enough to get you going. Some people feel that the potential of podcasting has only scratched the surface. The uses that they can be put to is almost unlimited, such as: training or how to fix, maintain, or upgrade almost anything, from diesel engines to high-end electronics. Imagine having a video cast showing you how to do something, while you are listening to the explanation. Consider our lawnmower example where we sharpened the blade. Then imagine complex maintenance to a jet aircraft, nuclear submarine, or the computer in your car. The future of podcasting may really be unlimited.

Digital Photography

11

There is a lot of information here surrounding digital photography, but nothing is more important than making high-quality pictures that accomplish their purpose. So let's start with that.

You can produce high-quality pictures consistently. Making high-quality pictures is no different from making any other high-quality product. As with all else in life, practice makes perfect. The more pictures you make the faster and easier you will make them. If you make few pictures they may not be as good as someone who shoots pictures all the time. To help you around that we will share a technique that will having you making better pictures instantly—yes, it's that good (more about that later). Before we go much further, never put a picture on the Web unless it performs a valid function and it contains a caption (unless the purpose is obvious). You need to place words with the photo so the reader can quickly and easily see why the picture is there and what it is showing the reader. Do not place pictures, or graphics, on your Web site without a valid reason. To do so just confuses people.

What Makes a Good Picture

Any good picture has these qualities. (One caveat to my artistic friends: None of what I have here applies to a work of art. When your aim is art, and not descriptive informative, commercially viable work, these things go out the window.) Here we are making photography that needs to accomplish a non-artistic purpose and must be recognizable on a Web page. Your picture needs to be:

❯ Sharply focused. Absolutely razor sharp.

❯ Well exposed; no black areas that are bullet proof. No overexposed areas that are totally white, not even when the subject is white. This includes snow.

❯ Well composed. The subject of the photograph dominates the picture. There is a very great difference between a picture of someone standing on a beach and a picture of the person. When the person is tiny and the beach is huge it is not a picture of a person on the beach. It is a picture of a beach with a person standing on it. Not the same thing at all.

Making high-quality pictures

Contrary to popular belief, you do not start with the camera. Actually taking the picture is not the first, and only step. No, first you set up the shot. Doing this right is what separates those who know what they are doing from those whose total photographic equipment is a camera. Let's stay with our example of taking someone's picture, say, a portrait. Here are some typical steps:

1. Make an appointment with the person to be photographed, so he or she arrives ready and dressed for the occasion.

2. Be sure the camera battery is fully charged, and that there is enough memory available to hold 20 or so high-resolution pictures. The resolution you choose is associated with the purpose of the picture. High resolution for making a print. Low resolution is fine for the Web. We recommend making all of your pictures in high resolution, so that later the picture can be printed if need be.

3. Have your studio setting ready. Are you using lights? If so, they must be set up, plugged in, or fully charged, and ready to go. Are you using a window for lighting? Does the window have sheer curtains? They are an excellent diffuser that create superb portrait lighting.

4. Do you have a dog or cat? Be sure that Rover and Kitty are not around.

5. Talk to the subject of the portrait. Put him or her at ease. If your person likes the Yankees, you like the Yankees. This is not the place for discussions that can lead to disagreements. Happy faces make nice photographic faces.

6. Need additional light to fill shadows under the chin? A book will do the job. Open the book; its white pages make an excellent reflector.

7. Use a tripod.

8. When using multiple electronic flash heads you have got to know what you are doing, and have an electronic flash meter to calculate the exposure.

9. The portrait's composition. You have several possibilities:

    ❯ A head and shoulders picture

    ❯ A shot from the waist up

    ❯ A full-figure portrait

    Each of these have advantages and disadvantages. Choose based on what the picture will be used for. For an About Us page, a head shot or a head and shoulders shot looks great.

10. Compose and take numerous photographs.

11. On camera flash can be a disaster. If your pictures include red-eye you will need to remove it later with your graphics engine.

12. When using off camera flash, practice before the formal shoot to check for shadows. Look carefully under the eyes, under the chin. Is there a hard shadow that follows the subject's head on the background? You can remove it later in your digital darkroom, but it takes time. Sometimes lots of time. Fix problems in the camera whenever possible.

Okay, you can see that taking the picture, actually using the camera, is not the big bite here. It is usually not in professional photography. Working with people, controlling lighting, setting up the composition, and making sure that the final needs of the photograph are addressed require more than simply taking a grab shot.

Seeing the final result before you make the photo

This technique works. I've used it for years, and have taught it in many classes. It will make the next picture you take better. It is what I call "running your eye around the viewfinder."

Works like this. You look through the viewfinder, or at the LCD display, and now start looking at the picture. Start at the bottom "run" your eye around the viewfinder. Is there a tree growing out of someone's head? Move and recompose the shot. Is there a garbage can on the right? Zoom in, take a step or two to the left. Look at your subject. Is he chewing gum? Get rid of the gum. By solving problems before they become pictures you improve the picture tremendously before it is even taken. Learn; take the time to learn to see what you are photographing. The camera is telling you a story. Learn to see what the camera is showing you. This is what artists and photographers call learning to see. They don't mean seeing like reading a book. They mean in the sense of being aware of what you are producing. Okay, now that you are on your way to seeing the picture before you take it, your photography just improved 10,000 percent.

As this is a book largely dedicated to text, let's assume that you are either the writer taking pictures, or taking pictures to support the writer. Either way, you know that your pictures will be used to illustrate written matter online, or maybe not online. Knowing ahead of time what the photos will be used for is critical to your success.

The quick guide to superior pictures

» Line up the camera so that walls and other vertical structures are as close to vertical as you can make them.

» Try not to shoot into the sun, or other bright light source.

» Compose your pictures with a little "extra room" around the subject so you can crop to size later.

» Get close. Make the subject of the picture dominate the image.

» Get to know and be friends with the camera's flash. Using your flash during the day to fill shadows can reduce the time needed for digital editing later.

» You may hear the terms *burning* and *dodging*. To burn is to add light or lighten an area of a picture. To dodge is to reduce the light or to darken a portion of a photograph. Why are we telling you this? Graphics engines have a burn/dodge tool. Now you know what it is for. The GIMP, the free graphics engine, has a terrific tool for this that we just love.

When all else fails: Digital retouching

This is done with a graphics engine. We will mention three here; there are others of course. Here are three graphics engine you can check out (in alphabetical order):

» The GIMP, *www.gimp.org*. The GNU image manipulation program that they, the GNU folks, give away for free. The GIMP is good stuff.

» PaintShopPro, *www.jasc.com*.

» Photoshop, by Adobe. Download it here: *www.photoshop.s0ftware-now.com*.

All of these will work fine with a Wacom tablet, *www.wacom.com*, which is also a terrific device. We love ours.

When editing a picture make small changes and adjustments. If you make a mess of the picture, do not save it. Let's repeat that: **Do not** save it. Best of all is that these graphics engines can take your picture back in time to how it was before you destroyed it. This feature is easy to do, and, yes, we use it all the time. While we are talking about editing, never edit or change an original picture—just don't do it. Rather, open the picture in your graphics engine and save it under another name. Then edit the second picture. It is after all an identical copy of the first picture. This way, to get back to where you began all you do is reopen the original picture and you are right back where you began. This is a very old IT trick, and not just for graphics either: Never edit original material, no matter what it is. Always copy it to another file, rename it, and edit the copy.

When you wish to use something like a thumbnail, or a small photograph, that the user can see and decide if he or she wants to click for a larger view, here is the way to handle that. Open the picture in a graphics engine and make two pictures. The first is thumbnail size, say 1 inch high or so. The second is larger, say 3 inches high or so. Now place the thumbnail as a link and have the link open the larger picture. By making an actual small image as the thumbnail you avoid the noise, or artifacts, that result from making an image smaller by using the height and width attributes of the HTML image tag.

Putting Your Pictures on the Web

Now that you have a digital image Web-ready, how do you make it show up on your Web site? Funny you should ask. You use the image tag. It looks like this, and has numerous attributes, all of which we will discuss here.

<img src="filename" alt=" " height=" " width=" " hspace=" " vspace=" " align=" ">

All your tags go between the < (the less than character) and the > (greater than character) characters. You knew that.

img = image

src = source

filename = is the name of the graphics file.

align= top, bottom, middle, left, right

alt= " " is where you include text that appears in any Web browser that can't show the graphic.

height= " " is where you control the height of the graphic file

width= " " is where you control the width of the graphics file

hspace= " " controls the amount of space horizontally that is left and right of the image

vspace= " " controls the space that is vertically or to top and bottom of the image.

So let's look at a tag that puts the file cat.jpg on your Web site. It might look like this:

<img src=cat.jpg> that would do it. If you want it on the right side of the page, add the align attribute, like this: <img src=cat.jpg align= right>. Now the graphic is on the right side of the screen. To let people know that this is a picture of a cat, should their browser not show images, use that alt attribute:

<img src=cat.jpg align=right alt="This is my cat.">.

Okay, except you have some text and the text is too close to the picture and you don't like that. So let's use hspace and vspace to put some room around our cat, like this:

<img src=cat.jpg align=right alt="This is my cat." hspace="10px" vspace="10px">.

Now you have 10 pixels of space on top, bottom, left, and right of the picture of our cat. This forms a buffer around the image that is 10 pixels wide. This looks much better and you are happy.

What about height and width? We do not recommend that you use them for anything but small changes in image size. One of our clients had trouble with pictures on his site. He took them at high resolution and showed them at about 1 inch high and 1 inch wide. This deforms the image, making it look lumpy. To be technically correct it creates artifacts that do not look good. Especially when you are selling what you are taking pictures of. To solve this problem make two photographs: one small and the other large. Make the small one a hypertext link that opens the larger picture. Put the large photograph in its own widow with a link that closes the window when clicked, or make the large photograph a clickable link that closes the window when clicked. Be sure to put some words onscreen so the user knows to click the photograph. This works great.

How Many Pixels Are Enough?

As digital camera manufactures tout the number of Megapixels, millions of pixels, in their cameras it is only right that you should think this is important. And it is, but only so far. The total number of pixels is determined like this: A resolution of 1,280 by 1,024 is 1,310,720, which is 1,280 multiplied by 1,024. Or the image contains 1,310,720 pixels.

At some point another million pixels no longer improve the picture. This was shown by tests at CNET. Of course, more pixels don't hurt, but that is not the only consideration relating to picture quality. As in film photography, the quality of the lens also plays a leading role.

Resolution of Digital Images

Resolution is measured in pixels per inch or, as pixels are more commonly referred to, dots per inch, or simply dpi. A graphic image's resolution is measured by its width and height in pixels. For example, a picture might be 640 by 480, meaning 640 pixels by 480 pixels.

The higher the resolution of an image the more pixels the image contains and the better its quality will be. Also, a high-quality picture with lots of pixels will consume a great deal of memory when saved and be slow to download as all that information must be transmitted to the user.

This is especially important when you are designing content for the World Wide Web. Pixels, short for picture elements, are the individual dots you see on your computer monitor. In fact your monitor is made up of thousands of these tiny colored points of light.

It is important to note that device resolution, such as that of a printer or monitor, is the maximum number of dots per inch, dpi, the device can produce. Monitors vary between 60 and 120 dpi; printers vary greatly.

Some resolutions for different applications

Images in a Newsletter:	400 by 300 dpi
World Wide Publishing:	640 by 480 dpi
Video Slides:	640 by 480 dpi
Photographs you perceive to be very high quality:	1,280 by 1,024 dpi
Web publishing:	73 dpi

While we may like the look of graphics on a computer monitor—and yes, they do look good—the quality of a image that looks great on a monitor would be absolutely putrid should the picture be printed at, say, 73 dpi. So, be advised, that on the Web 73dpi is fine, but not for anything that is to be printed or used as hard copy.

Taking the Picture

Digital photography, like anything else, can benefit from some basis do's and don'ts. So here are a few:

> ❧ Do not rely on the digital zoom, if you can help it. Why? The digital zoom magnifies the pixels in the image. It is not the same as a zoom lens. The digital zoom actually gives you a picture of lower quality than a picture taken with no digital zoom. Get close to the subject whenever you can.

❯ The Liquid Crystal Diode (LCD) viewfinder is a battery hog. Use it sparingly. Instead use the camera's optical viewfinder to compose the photo. Also, holding the camera at arm's length to see the LCD display can create unsharp photos, as the camera is more apt to shake.

❯ The flash on your digital camera may not be very powerful, so know and stay in its working range or your photographs may be dark. See the documentation that came with your camera and look up the effective range of the flash.

❯ Do use rechargeable batteries and a charger rather than throw away batteries. The money you save will easily pay for the batteries and charger.

❯ Do have extra memory. Always bring extra memory when you will be doing a large job. While we are talking about memory chips, they are delicate. Only remove and handle them where it is safe to do so. Pictures on a damaged card may not be recoverable.

❯ It is likely that your camera will make photographs that are 12, 20, or even 40 inches wide. These pictures are far too large to place on the Web. Do use your graphics engine to resize them to a smaller size. When you save the resized image, do not overwrite the original picture. Save the smaller picture with the letters *-sm* at the end of the file name. Like this: car.jpg when made smaller will be car-sm.jpg. This way when both pictures are in the same directory you can see quickly which pictures have been resized and which ones have not because the -sm.jpg files will sort just after the files without the -sm letters in their file names.

Digital graphic file formats

Some file formats, like JPEG, use lossy algorithms. The term *lossy* means that every time you change, or edit, the picture, you lose some detail. To avoid this loss of detail copy your lossy file into the native format of the graphics engine you are using. That will be a TIFF, or another non-lossy, file format. Edit the TIFF, or other native format file, and then save it as a JPEG.

Many pictures and graphics on the Web are either GIF or JPG format. In general use GIF for graphics and JPG for pictures.

After you make all these beautiful photos you will want to save them for future use. There are several file formats to choose from so it is in your best interest to know something about the various formats.

» **Bit Map.** One of the three classes that graphic files are found in. Bit map, meta file, and vector. A bit mapped graphic is composed of a collection if individual dots, or pixels. The simplest bit mapped files are monochromes composed of only black and white pixels.

» **CGM** (Computer Graphics Meta File). A vector graphics format designed to be portable from one Windows or DOS program to the next.

» **EPS, EPSF** (Encapsulated Post Script Format). This meta file format for graphics contains two elements: the bit mapped image and the PostScript code that tells your printer, or other output device, how to print the graphic.

» **GIF** (Graphic Interchange Format). This is a standard format for images created by CompuServe so that users could exchange images online. GIF format is an 8 bit per pixel format. That means that a GIF can have 256 or fewer colors in an image, which is very useful for line drawings and cartoons. GIF files can be animated or have transparent backgrounds. This allows the background color of the Web page to be seen rather than the background for the GIF. Think of this as if the graphic is on glass. You see through the glass to the background of the Web site. Here is an example of a transparent GIF versus a non-transparent GIF. The transparent gif is on the left; non-transparent on the right. You can see that the background color (white) "shows through" the transparent GIF, while the non-transparent GIF has a blueish background. These images have a border added, the border is not part of the image, so you can plainly see that the transparent GIF truly takes on the background color of the document. With the transparent GIF you cannot determine where the graphic ends and the background of the page begins, unless you use a border, that is. See page 70 for an example of a transparent graphic.

» **HDF** (Hierarchical Data Format). A format type to transfer graphic numerical data between machines.

❯ Indexed Color. These files are of two types: those with a limited number of colors and pseudo color images. The first type usually have 256 colors and are adequate for the Web. Pseudo color images are gray scale that display variations in gray levels in color rather than shades of gray. They are typically used in scientific and technical work and can be referred to as false color images.

❯ JPEG or JPG (Joint Photographic Experts Group). JPEG is designed to store real-world images like landscapes and other natural scenes. Using a 24 bit storage format JPEG can record 16,777,216 colors. These files are not necessarily larger in file size than GIF images. JPEG uses a lossy algorithm to do its data compression. What that means to you is that when compressed data is lost and it cannot be recovered. This loss is designed to affect irregularities too slight for the human eye to notice easily. Be safe and save your original pictures and edit copies of the original in TIFF, or a similar format. When you have the edited picture the way you want it then save it to JPEG format. But, as always, save all originals files as they are. It is not a good idea to change an original. Make copies and do your editing on the copy.

❯ Meta File. This format supports vector and bit mapped date within the same file. While popular in the Windows environment, Apples PICT format does the same thing.

❯ PCD. Photo CD.

❯ PCX. This does not mean anything, as it was originally developed to support the PC Paintbrush program. You will find that most Windows and DOS graphics programs read and write PCX files.

❯ PDF (Portable Document Format). This format was developed by Adobe and is designed for the use of graphics, fonts, and color for electronically accessed documents. To use this you need a viewer.

❯ PICT. A PICT file contains bit map and vector data. These are excellent for importing and printing black and white graphics. The term *PICT* is a meaningless acronym.

❯ PostScript. This is a programming language that defines the shapes in a file as outlines and then interprets the outlines using a mathematical formula called Bézier curves.

❯ Raster. See Bit Map.

❯ TIFF (Tagged Image File Format). Developed by Microsoft and Aldus for use in scanners and desktop publishing. You will find that this is usually supported by external viewers.

❯ Vector. A vector file is defined in terms of shapes. Each file is a mathematical description of the shapes that compose the graphic and are sometimes called object oriented. The same technology that is used in PostScript fonts is used here and has the same advantage—namely, that you can make any image as large as you want and it will retain its quality. Vector files are displayed as a bit map.

❯ WMF (Windows Meta File Format). A vector graphics format designed to be portable from one Windows application to the next.

APPENDICIES

APPENDIX A

Grammar

Grammar is the set of rules or a road map, if you will, defining how we get from here to there using the written word. Without grammar it would be chaos out there. There is no way to make you an expert grammarian, so let's discuss three important members of our punctuation family.

Modifiers

Adverbs and adjectives are modifiers. They modify, describe, enhance, increase, decrease, or alter the meaning of other words, but offer no additional information. Avoid modifiers if at all possible. Rather than use them opt for language that conveys meaning and not just modification that may or may not be understood by the user. They often end in the letters *ly*. You may see something described as "really fast." Just what does that mean? To the user it means one thing and to you the writer it may mean something entirely different. Rather than say that a motor cycle is "really fast" it is far better to say that it will go from 0 to 60 miles per hour in four seconds. Do not leave out the miles per hour, or mph. You do not want people asking if you refer to mph or kph, kilometers per hour.

In general using words that end in *ly* are a poor way to describe something. This is true online and in print. Try not do use them in your description. While you know what you are talking about and the message you are trying to get across, the user does not.

When you write descriptions about products, opinions, or materials with which you are not familiar, get people involved who are. Your text must be targeted to users in such a manner that they can understand it and it must be backed up with facts showing that your description is accurate. Do not expect users to know. Remember the advertiser's maxim: Tell them, tell them what you told them, tell them again. To that we add: Back up what you tell people with facts so that they know, in no uncertain terms.

Punctuation

1. The period [.] is used to end a sentence and to indicate that letters have been intentionally left out (words have been abbreviated). For example:

   ❯ a.m. or A.M. refers to ante meridian, or before noon.

   ❯ Dr. refers to Doctor.

   ❯ Mr. refers to Mister.
   Note: *Messrs* is used when referring to more than one man. For example Messrs Thompson, Brown, and Smith.

2. The comma [,]

   ❯ Set apart introductory words.

   For example: As we were saying, this fuel is fine for your needs.

   ❯ Separate items in a series of three or more.

   For example: The cars are available in **red, green, white, black, and green.**
   Note: Some writers omit the comma before the second-to-the-last item. Hence: The cars are available in red, green, white, black and green. Note however, that this may create confusion. Are the cars painted black and green in two tone? Or are some cars completely green and others completely black? Do not force the user to decipher your content.

   ❯ Enclose parenthetic expressions.

   For example: **This meter, available for the first time,** is excellent for your needs.

   ❯ Place a comma before a conjunction introducing an independent clause.

   For example: The situation is serious, but there is a chance we can still survive. [comma before *but* and other words; for example, *for, or, nor, while*]

   ❯ When writing day and date.

   For example: The event will be held on Tuesday, July 1, 2008, at 8 a.m. Or use 24-hour time, 08:00, if appropriate. Give users complete day, date, and time-of-day information.

3. The apostrophe [']

   ❯ Used to form the possessive singular:

For example: John's car. The car belongs to John. Never, Johns' car. As this indicates that the car is owned by numerous people all named John.

4. The colon [:]

   ❯ The colon can be translated—as follows—and indicates that the following text relates closely.

   For example: The car is currently composed of: engine, wheels, and transmission.

   ❯ For our purposes the colon can be used to introduce a numbered or unnumbered list.

   For example:
   Don't forget to bring:

   · Your toothbrush

   · Toothpaste

   · Pajamas

   · A comb

   · Nail clippers

5. The semi colon [;]

   ❯ Join two independent clauses with a semicolon.

   For example: The Web site is super; it contains a vast amount of excellent data.

   ❯ Also, for our purposes it can be used to separate a long string of information where the continued use of commas would be confusing. This is an excellent technique and well worth remembering.

   For example: The tour will play in: Boston, MA; New York, NY; Miami, FL; Los Angeles, CA; and Dallas, TX.

Common Mistakes

1. Its and it's:

   a. *It's* is a contraction meaning *it is.*

   b. *Its* is a possessive. A wise dog scratches its own fleas.

2. Use an before words that have vowel sounds

   a. An apple

   b. An itch

3. A is used before consonant sounds

   a. A truck

   b. A plane

Spelling and Typographical Errors

Never trust your computer's dictionary. It is a good place to start, but cannot be relied upon. The reason why, of course, is that it can not determine a correctly spelled word that is not the right word.

For example: This goatee ate ice scream.
All words are spelled correctly. There is no defense against the wrong word that is spelled correctly except human proofreading. So proofread.

Bus and buss. A bus is a conveyance for moving people, or other things, from place to place. A buss is a kiss. Children ride in a bus, not a buss.

Weather is rainy, warm, or cold. **Wether** is a castrated ram. Proofread.

The best way to eliminate typographical errors and misspellings is to:

❯ Print the material and read it out loud.

❯ Read the material backward.

❯ Put it down for a day or two and then read it again.

❯ Have someone else read it.

Some typographical errors (typos) are of far greater consequence than others. To misspell a common word is embarrassing, but of little import. To misspell your boss's name is a problem. To publish an incorrect date for an event is a disaster.

Do not place information on the Web if there is any chance that it could change in a meaningful way. To correct misinformation can be a significant problem, create red faces, and make real trouble for those who rely on what turns out to be bad data. This is especially true for the date, time, and place of an event. When making significant changes both old and new information can be shown. This way the user can see what it was and what it is now. This avoids questions, e-mails, and phone calls.

APPENDIX B

A Writer's Checklist

☐ 1. Has the client approved the content? This is especially true for first-time content.

☐ 2. Never use pictures that contain recognizable people, and especially children, without written permission. When you need pictures use an online stock photo house and purchase them if necessary. Include a disclaimer on the About Us page mentioning that the pictures are purchased for the purpose of being on the Web.

☐ 3. Know how to use grammar, especially commas and quotation marks. John said, "He lives in the red house on the corner." The period goes inside the quotation marks. Look for words that sound the same, but are nothing alike: *Your* house is lovely. *You're* lucky to live there.

☐ 4. Spell-check all your material. Relentlessly hunt down typographical errors and misspellings.

☐ 5. Use exclamation marks sparingly. They are rarely justified and usually overused. Please, only one at a time, if at all. Write your prose so that it indicates urgency. Place the immediacy, danger, importance in your text.

☐ 6. Grammar and spelling must be correct and proper. If you have questions, buy and read *The Elements of Style* by Strunk and White.

☐ 7. Look for:

    a. All sentences must express a complete thought. Every sentence must indicate what is done, who or what does it, and the action. John ran across the street.

b. Each sentence must contain a verb—the word *ran* in "John ran across the street." The verb is the action and it must agree with the subject. "They are going home" is correct; "Bob are going home" is wrong. End sentences with a period or other appropriate punctuation.

c. Are you using the correct plurals for your nouns and pronouns? They must agree with the rest of the sentence. Don't say, "These car are the fastest around" when you mean, "These cars are the fastest around."

d. Commas, when properly used, can make your writing clear. Know how to use them. Always write for clarity. Do whatever it takes to turn out prose that is understood for its intended purpose.

e. When you need to show who or what owns something, use an apostrophe. "John's house is on the corner." Never write, "Johns' house is on the corner." This indicates that more than one person named John lives there.

f. Paragraphs are to be indented. They are more easily read that way and give a visual cue that helps break up text. Also, people are used to seeing indented paragraphs in newspapers, magazines, books. It is what users expect and look for; don't disappoint them.

g. Proper nouns and the first word of a sentence need to be capitalized. Do not write, "the truck was made by gm." When you mean, "The truck was made by GM."

APPENDIX C

Web Design and HTML

While design is the province of the Web master it is in your best interest to voice opinions and concerns before the design is finalized. When changes affect the way you will present material, you need to say so. This is especially true when changes will add significant time to your efforts that have not been budgeted in the project. Don't think you can bury the time elsewhere in the project; you can't. Trying to do so will only embarrass you and hurt your reputation when you are asked why something took longer than expected. That is not the time to say that a redesign hurt your schedule.

Example of poor presentation

The Aperture or f-stop

The aperture had been known to strike terror in the hearts of all but the most stalwart shutterbug. All those little weird nmbers, they must mean something to somebody. Well, here is a surprise, because f-stops are really quite simple. In fact the f-stop isn't a thing at all. It's a relationship between the focal length of the lens and the lens diameter. As the lens diameter changes the f-stop changes.

The f-stop, or aperture, controls the intensity of the light reaching the film or digital sensor. It does this by acting like a window blind. Open the aperture and more light passes through the lens. Close the aperture and less light passes through. It is just that simple.

Let's talk about window blinds. Blinds admit more light when open ½ of maximum than when open ¼ of maximum, in this same way, f2, is larger than f4. Yes, f2 means that the aperture is one-half the focal length, f4 means that the aperture is one-fourth of the focal length.

In terms we all understand, dollars and cents, one-half dollar more that one-quater of a dollar. So, f2 is larger than f4. It really is just that simple. A half dollar is more than a quarter of a dollar, amazing how simple it is when we relate it to money, is it not?

The adjustment for the f-stop is located on the lens barrel. It will be marked with numbers such as:

1.2, 1.4, 1.7, 1.8, 2.0, 2.8, 3.5, 4,5.6, 8, 11, 16, 22, 32, etc.

Example of good presentation

The Aperture or f-stop

The f-stop, or aperture, controls the intensity of the light reaching the film or digital sensor. It does this by acting like a window blind.

Open the aperture and more light passes through the lens. Close the aperture and less light passes through. It is just that simple.

Let's talk about window blinds. Blinds admit more light when open ½ of maximum than when open ¼ of maximum, in this same way, f2, is larger than f4. Yes, f2 means that the aperture is one-half the focal length, f4 means that the aperture is one-fourth of the focal length.

In terms we all understand, dollars and cents, one-half dollar is more that one-quater of a dollar. So, f2 is larger than f4.

It really is just that simple. A half dollar is more than a quarter of a dollar. Amazing how simple it is when we relate it to money, is it not?

The adjustment for the f-stop is located on the lens barrel. It will be marked with numbers such as:

1.2, 1.4, 1.7, 1.8, 2.0, 2.8, 3.5, 4,5.6, 8, 11, 16, 22, 32, etc.

How to Begin a Web Page

When dealing with any client we suggest that you provide opening text for every page of their Web site. Each page should be started with a unique title that is identifies he page and its contents to the user. You can be sure that the Web master will have unique page names for all files.

Recommended Fonts and Font Size

Fonts come in two varieties. Those with serifs and those that are non-serif (sans serif). Serif fonts have sharp endings on their letters. Non-serif fonts are more squared off. *This font is Times New Roman.* You can see that the S has rather sharp endings.

We recommend Times New Roman, Arial, Verdana, and Georgia. A font of 12 points is fine. *This sentence is in 12 point font.* Headings are **bold**.

Text color, size, and font face will likely be chosen for you by the Webmaster. If you are free to choose, use the font, point size, and color listed here.

Avoid using unusual fonts, italics, bolding, or CAPITALIZING all of your text. Likewise, avoid changing the color of the text. Your site wants to present a consistent look.

Stay away from exotic fonts. While thay may look nice on your development computer, you can not be sure that the user's machine will be able to display them. Also, they can be hard to read as these fonts show.

When you need to use fonts like this for a logo or page heading use a graphics engine to create a GIF image.

Edwardian Script ITC
Edwardian Script ITC

Kristen ITC
Kristen ITC

Parchment
Parchment

Juice ITC
Juice ITC

Magneto
Magneto

BREMEN BD BT
Bremen BD BT

Foreground and Background Color

Foreground color refers to the color of your text.

Background refers to the color of the page itself.

In this document the text is black and the background is white. Black text on white background has been used for centuries. There is a reason for that: It's easy to read. Avoid color schemes that do not provide maximum contrast. Always maintain high contrast between your text and the background color of the page. Navy blue text on white or a light yellow background is a fine combination and easy on the eyes.

There are Web sites that will actually give you a headache from reading them because the text and background colors do not make sufficient contrast. Your users will go elsewhere if your site gives them a headache. Wouldn't you?

Photographs, Graphics, and Charts

Your text and graphics should compliment each other.

1. Keep photographs and graphics 73dpi (dots per inch). Photographs should be used for a definite purpose and include a caption so the user can determine the photograph's relevance and how the photograph fits into the information that is being presented.

2. Use a high-quality digital SLR (Single Lens Reflex) camera if at all possible.

3. Focus critically.

4. The exposure must be proper for what you are trying to show. Do not use photos that are too light or dark.

5. Be aware of the background and minimize any distractions from the main point that you are using the photograph to highlight.

6. Choose photographs that are easily recognized and that have a purpose relevant to the text. The subject of the photograph must dominate the picture.

7. Insert the date the photo was made in the file name of the picture. This way you, or your Web master, can easily determine when how old it is.

8. Photographs must be sharply focused and well exposed.

9. Do not use large image files and then make them smaller on the users screen. Rendering a large picture as a small one will not reduce its download time. Open large pictures in a graphics engine and resize them.

10. Should you wish users to be able to print out high quality pictures. You will need to offer 200 or 300 dpi images. These pictures will require longer download time.

We teach photography. There is no excuse for poor quality pictures. Well, no good excuse.

Graphs and charts benefit from the same comments as for photos. Be sure that your graphs and charts have their axes and titles clearly and meaningfully titled. Never expect the user to know or guess what the graph refers to.

Here you can see the benefit of using a table to present information. The paragraph shown here contains all of the data that the table on page 199 does. As you can see, the table presents the material in a far more readable format.

Bob, Fred, Tom, Dick, Pete, and Jim are gamers and have lots of computers. Bob has an Alienware, Fred has an IBM, Tom has a Dell, Dick has a Mac, Pete's is homemade, and Jim has an HP. The Alienware has 4 Gig of RAM, the IBM has 2 Gig RAM, the Dell has 4.5 Gig, the Mac has 1.5 Gig RAM, the homemade has 4 Gig RAM, and the HP has 2 Gig RAM. The Alienware has 1 Gig on the video board. The IBM has 512 on the video board, the Dell has 256 on the video board, the Mac has 1 Gig on the video board, the homemade has 2 Gig on the video board, and the HP has 512 on the video board. The Alienware has 500 Gig on the hard drive. The IBM has 120 Gig hard drive, the Dell has 160 Gig hard drive. The Mac has 500 Gig hard drive. The homemade has 1000 Gig hard drive, and the HP has 160 Gig hard drive.

Owner	Make	RAM	Video Board Memory	Hard Drive Capacity
Bob	Alienware	4 Gig	1 Gig	500 Gig
Fred	IBM	2 Gig	512K	120 Gig
Tom	Dell	4.5 Gig	256K	160 Gig
Dick	Mac	1 Gig	1 Gig	500 Gig
Pete	Homemade	4 Gig	2 Gig	1000 Gig
Jim	HP	2 Gig	512K	160 Gig

Links and Formatting of Title Information

By using a few commands you can actually insert blank lines and additional spaces into a link's title. You will use these codes:

❥ for a line feed: &#10

❥ for a blank space:

Place these codes inside the title's quotations marks.

<a href=http://www.webaddress.com title='This is information on the link and will pop up when the mouse is placed on the link.
This text is on a new line.'>Link description</a>

To include a link that will place the URL of a site into the Favorites List of the user's computer use this script:

<script language="JavaScript1.2">

var bookmarkurl="http://www.WebAddress.com"

var bookmarktitle="Title text goes here."

function addbookmark(){

if (document.all)

window.external.AddFavorite(bookmarkurl,bookmarktitle)

</SCRIPT>

APPENDIX D

Your Business

Okay, we know this is a book on Web content. So what are we doing digressing into this stuff? Well, hey, you are in business to make money. And making money can be a real serious thing when you need to use the money you need to pay the rent, buy food, and do other things that can not be ignored. So, here are a few words on the business end of the business. In general, there is one thing you should always do. Actually, this is easy because it is really doing nothing. Spend no time on a job unless you have a contract or letter of agreement signed. Sure, you need to talk to people and e-mail them and, yes, of course you must spend time to capture the business, but do not begin the job until you have it signed, sealed, and delivered. Once the work is in the bag, go to it. Until then, work on other things.

A Sample Contract

There are contracts everywhere and we will also include one for you that we use for big jobs. Although, we must say that a letter of agreement works just fine. Here is a contract. Do not use it until you have had a lawyer approve it. This contract is for your perusal only. It is not to be considered a legal document and using it without a lawyer's approval is not recommended.

Do Not Use This Document Without Approval
From Your Lawyer.

CONTRACT

Your Business Name

and

Client

THIS AGREEMENT, made and entered into on this the _____ day of _____, by and between CLIENT and *Your Business Name* is to witness the following. The parties agree as follows:

1.   TERM

a.   The term of the agreement shall be from the DATE until DATE.

2.   SERVICES

a.   YourBusinessName agrees to prepare a PROJECT for CLIENT. See Scope of the Project, below. YourBusinessName shall work approximately XX hours per week. If more hours are requires they shall be approved by CLIENT.

3.   CHARGES

a.   All hours spent on this project will be billed at $_____ (write out dollars) per hour.

b.   YourBusinessName will invoice CLIENT every two weeks, and CLIENT shall pay invoice withing 15 days of receipt.

c.   Work will not continue if any invoice is not paid withing 15 days.

d.   Prepayment is required for delivery of the final installment of the project. YourBusinessName will withhold delivery of the final 15% of the project until the final invoice is paid in full.

4.   TERMINATION

a.   This agreement may be terminated at any time before the completion of the agreement upon five (5) days prior written notice. Upon termination of the agreement by either party, CLIENT shall pay YourBusinessName for any hours worked for which YourBusinessName has not already invoiced CLIENT, plus any unpaid hours.

b.   This contract may be cancelled by either party by means of a written notice.

5.   SCOPE OF THE PROJECT

a.   Insert as much detail as possible

6.   ESTIMATE OF TIME TO COMPLETE PROJECT

a.   **THIS IS ONLY AN ESTIMATE**. The actual time required to complete this project may include changes unforseen in this estimate. Those unknown costs, if any, are not included and will be invoiced at the hourly rate.

b.   Based on the Scope of the Project, as it appears above, this project is estimated at XXX hours to research, write, edit, print, and convey to client.

c.   YourBusinessName will bill the client for hours worked. This estimate in no way reflects the total number of hours that may be spent on this project SHOULD THE CLIENT CHANGE THE Scope of the Project.

7.   CHANGE REQUESTS

a.   Change Requests may require additional time and may increase the cost of the project.

b.   Changes Requests are best made in writing.

c.   Telephone Change Requests shall be followed up by YourBusinessName via email or letter delivered by US Post, if the customer does not use email. All time for these administrative activities will be invoiced to the client at the hourly rate. Further, Change Request(s) submitted by telephone shall be approved by signature of the client or the clients representative. All telephone Change Requests will be placed on a list and this lint sent to the client or the clients representative for approval by signature.

8.   COPYRIGHT

a.   YourBusinessName retains the copyright to all written materials in this project until the project is paid in full.

b.   No part or section or this material may be used in whole or in part in any form or placed on an information retrieval system, on a computer, the World Wide Web, in any electronic form, print, CD-ROM, DVD, on Television, or in any other media, in any way until YourBusinessName has been paid in full for this project.

9.   TECHNICAL ACCURACY

a.   All material of a technical or proprietary nature will be proof read by the client for accuracy and correctness.

b.   YourBusinessName is not responsible for errors, omissions, or other inaccuracies in this material.

c.   YourBusinessName will be notified of any edits that need to be made before final project material is delivered to the client.

10.   CONFIDENTIALITY

a.   YourBusinessName agrees not to disclose information relating to the products, trade secrets, methods of manufacturing, or business affairs of CLIENT that YourBusinessName may acquire in connection with or as a result of any work performed under this agreement. YourBusinessName will not, without prior written consent, publish, communicate, divulge, disclose, or use (except in the performance of the work specified in the agreement) any such information. This obligation of confidentiality shall not apply to information that:

i.   Becomes publically known through no fault of YourBusinessName.

ii.   CLIENT approves information or data for disclosure in a written document.

iii.   YourBusinessName rightfully possessed the information or data before disclosure by CLIENT, or

iv.   YourBusinessName independently developed information of data without the use of confidential information.

v.   Pertains to illegal activity or terrorism.

vi.   Pertains to sexual harassment, physical danger, or threats to the physical person of an employee, vendor, or other individual.

IN WITNESS WHEREOF, each party has caused this agree to be executed by its duly authorized representative on the date first mentioned above.

CLIENT warrants that it has full power and authority to enter into and perform this agreement, and that the person signing this agreement on CLIENT behalf has been duly authorized and empowered to enter into this agreement. CLIENT's and YourBusinessName further acknowledges that they have read this agreement, understand this agreement, and agree to be bound by this agreement.

_____

Your Business Name

Date _____

_____

Client or Client's Representative

Date _____

A Sample Letter of Agreement

Here the same holds true as what we said about contracts. We have had excellent luck using letters of agreement and recommend them. Here too, have it seen by your lawyer so that you have the legal protection that you demand.

TODAY'S DATE

Mr/Mrs/Ms Name of Client
Address of client

Dear: MR./MRS./MS. CLIENT

This letter confirms our contracting agreement as discussed on DATE.

We agreed that I would provide my services to CLIENT for the period between DATE and DATE. I will INSERT WHAT YOU WILL BE DOING. I will work approximately [XX] hours per week, more if necessary and if CLIENT approves the extra hours.

For my work CLIENT will pay me [$XX] an hour. I will invoice CLIENT every two weeks and CLIENT agrees to pay the invoice within 15 days of receipt.

This agreement may be terminated by either party at any time upon five days written notice. Upon termination, CLIENT will pay me for any hours that have I have worked for which I have not already invoiced CLIENT plus any unpaid invoices.

YOUR NAME is not responsible for the accuracy of financial, budgetary, or technical material submitted by CLIENT.

If this is your understanding of our agreement, please sign and date both copies of this letter, retain one and return the other to me. I look forward to working with you.
Sincerely,

YOUR NAME

Accepted by CLIENT:

Title: _____ Date: _____

Estimating the Job

No matter how you cut it, clients want to know how much a project will cost them. For small jobs—and you define small any way you want—fine, go ahead and give a total cost. We do not recommend that, but it is up to you. Why?

You work by the hour. The more hours the more you make. When you quote the entire job up front you are saying that the job will cost X amount and not more. To some people this is a license to steal. When you quote a job always include language something like this: This includes one edit. Additional edits will be billed at XX per hour.

Never, never, never (not ever) give a client the idea that you will just keep doing this over and over and over until they approve it. Companies are committees and to make my point a 747 jet airliner is a giraffe that was designed by a committee. Should you ever find that you need to satisfy numerous people and you can't. Well, guess what? Nobody else can either. Always report to one person.

Your Hourly Rate

Can't help you with this one. See what the going rate is for where you live, and, depending on your experience, adjust your rates accordingly. Sorry, best we can do.

APPENDIX E

A Short Style Guide and Confused Words

We present things that might be easily confused or written erroneously. This is by no means a complete style file. An excellent style book is the Associated Press Stylebook, *www.apstylebook.com*.

a.m., p.m. Lowercase, with periods. There is no need to add 10 a.m. this morning. It is redundant.

AM Amplitude Modulation. This refers to AM radio.

Bit. A bit is a binary digit and can have only the values of zero, 0, or one, 1. Binary information looks like this: 10010011. Here you have eight bits of binary information. A kilobit is 1,000 bits. A Megabit is one-million bits.

Byte. In most computers a byte is a unit of information that is eight bits in length. This can be used to indicate how much storage is available. For example, a 100-Megabyte hard drive will hold 100 Megabytes of information.

Cents. Spell out the word *cents* in lowercase. Use numerals for amounts lower than one dollar: 5 cents, 75 cents. Use the $ sign and decimal amount for larger amounts: $1.34, $14.23.

Dollars. The word *dollars* is written in lowercase except when the first word in a sentence. Use figures and the dollar sign ($) in all but the most casual and informal references.

> The singular verb is used to refer to any amount of money. "I know that $150 is what I owe him."
>
> For amounts greater than one million dollars use the $ sign and numerals and go to two decimal places. For example: $1.75 million. Do not use a hyphen to link the numerals and the word.
>
> For amounts less than $1 million use: $3, $25, $175, $1,000, $634,000.

Doughnut. Not donut.

Kilo. Refers to 1,000. A kilometer is 1,000 meters. A kilogram is 1,000 grams, written 1,000 g. In the world of computers kilo refers to 1,024, not 1,000. This comes from 2 raised to the tenth power, 2^{10}. Never confuse the two. A kilobyte is 1,024 bytes. A kilogram is 1,000 grams.

Mass and Weight. Weight is the measure of gravitational attraction. Take a brick into space and it has no, or little, weight. Mass measures the amount of matter in anything, be it a gas, a solid, or a liquid. Mass is measured in grams, kilograms, and metric tons. A metric ton is 1,000 kilograms. Weight is measured in ounces, pounds, and tons. A ton is 2,000 pounds. Never write that something has a weight of x grams. That is nonsense. In chemistry, when we speak of Atomic Weight, we are referring to Atomic Mass. Write weight like this: weight: 1 pound (454 grams). Never write weight: 10 grams. Grams do not measure weight.

Mega. One million. In distance or amounts of physical things it is 1,000,000 or one million. For example, one megawatt is one million watts. Shortened to uppercase M. As in 1 MW or 1,000,000 watts. In the world of computers mega refers to 1,048,576, not 1,000,000. This comes from 2 raised to the twentieth power, 2^{20}. Never confuse the two. A megabyte is 1,048,576 bytes. A megawatt is one million watts.

Numbers. Write out numbers less than 10. Use numbers for quantities greater than 10. There were four apples in the bag. The box contained 65 bolts. Write out large numbers such as 1.6 million rather than 1,600,000. Insert commas in large numbers: 1,600,000; never 1600000.

Money. See cents, dollars. When dealing with international currencies you can verify the spelling and current exchange rate online. Use any search engine to find a currency converter.

Temperature. There are four primary scales for measuring how warm things are are: Fahrenheit, Rankine, Celsius, and Kelvin. When writing a specific temperature write the amount, degrees, and the scale: 32 degrees Fahrenheit. Not 32 Fahrenheit degrees.

Note: When you wish to use the degree symbol, °, in a Web document, you may do so with the <sup> tag. You would write 32° F like this: 32° F.

Fahrenheit is the scale used in the United States. Water freezes at 32 degrees Fahrenheit and boils at 212 degrees Fahrenheit.

Rankine is an absolute temperature scale. Zero degrees Rankine is absolute zero. Water freezes at °491.67 ˜R and boils at 671.64 ˜R.

Celsius is the scale used in the metric system. Water freezes at 0° C (zero) degrees Celsius and boils at 100 degrees Celsius.

Kelvin is an absolute temperature scale. Water freezes at 273 degrees Kelvin and boils at 373 degrees Kelvin. Zero degrees Kelvin is absolute zero.

We suggest you use both Fahrenheit and Celsius by providing both temperatures: Water boils at 32° F (0° C).

Watt. A unit of power. 746 watts is one-horsepower.

Watt-hour. The use or generation of one watt for one hour. Usually seen as kilowatt-hour, meaning 1,000 watts-hours.

Word (computer related). In electronics and information technology a word is the number of bits that a computer reads. An 8-bit computer reads 8 bits at a time and has a word length of eight bits. A computer with a word length of 64 bits reads data in 64 bit chunks. Its word length is 64 bytes.

Commonly Confused Words

Accelerate/decelerate: *Accelerate* means to change the speed at which something is moving. Accelerate is commonly used to indicate that something speeds up, a due date is moved forward, or more progress needs to be made sooner. *Decelerate* is to slow something down or decrease the rate of progress.

We accelerated their education.

The car decelerated to 50 mph.

Accept/except: The verb *accept* means to receive something or to approve something. The preposition *except* means "other than" or "excluding."

I will be glad to accept your offer.

The report was fine except for the section on potatoes.

Advice/advise: The noun *advice* refers to a recommendation or opinions. The verb *advise* means to present those opinions or recommendations.

That is sound advice.

I will advise him to accept your plan.

Affect/effect: *Affect* as a verb means to influence. The results will affect how we do things. *Affect* as a noun is best avoided although it is sometimes used in psychology to refer to an emotion.

The mud affected (influenced) our operations.

The new drugs only effect (result) middle age men.

A lot: Do not write *a lot* as one word.

Already/all ready: Use *already* to indicate something previous to a time or event. Use two words to show that something is completely prepared.

The phone was already ringing when we got there.

Dinner is all ready.

All right: Do not write *all right* as one word.

Amount/number: Use *amount* when the quantity is unknown or cannot be counted. Use *number* when the quantity can be counted.

The train carried a large amount of grain.

The new technology offers a number of advantages.

Being as/being that: Do not use *being as* or *being that* in place of "because" or "since" to introduce a a dependant clause. Note: *Since* should be used in reference to time.

Because of the accident, our equipment was lost.

Since the tragic loss, she has not been the same.

Biweekly/bimonthly: These terms mean twice a week or month and every other week or month. This is confusing and readers will not know what you are referring to, so avoid using them.

Our newsletter is published every other week.

Can/may/might: *Can* is used to show that the ability to do something exists. Use *may* to show that permission needs to be obtained. *Might* shows uncertainty or that the situation may be contrary to actual fact.

The plane can fly for hours without refueling.

We may be able to upgrade the computer.

Having more people might have helped.

Continuous/continual: *Continuous* means to exist withour interruption or unceasing. *Continual* is to repeat or reoccur in rapid succession.

The road is continuous from here to the store.

The continual beeping drove everyone crazy.

Dashes to create a string of words with a specific meaning: When you use several words together to indicate a specific thought, definition, or concept connect them with dashes to indicate this to the reader.

over-the-counter drugs

They are sold over the counter.

a knock-your-socks-off plan

The plan will knock your socks off.

Data/datum: *Data* are given or admitted as a basis for inference or reasoning and is plural. *Datum* is singular; pluralize datum as data.

The data indicates that the car will break the sound barrier.

With only a single datum, we have little to go on.

E.g./i.e.: The abbreviation *e.g.* means "for example." It is an abbreviation of the Latin exempli gratia. Use *i.e.,* id est, to indicate "that is." These tend to confuse people. Avoid using them.

The new technology, i.e. the motor on a chip, is a cutting edge device.

We've updated our networking, e.g. our new server, and expect it to alleviate our communication bottleneck.

Flammable/inflammable: Both words indicate that the material in question, or something in general, is capable of burning. Safety experts prefer flammable because some people may read inflammable and believe that it will not burn. Use flammable.

Gasoline is flammable.

Imply/infer: *Imply* means to suggest without stating, and a writer or speaker may do that. To *infer* is to make a decision or extrapolate from facts (make a decision).

You may imply all you want, but there is no proof.

To infer, based on this meager data, is a mistake.

In, when used as a prefix: As a prefix indicates non or un. There are significant exceptions to this and we recommend the careful use of in, as a prefix.

Avoid inflammable because it means that something will burn. Always use flammable in your writing. Never use inflammable to indicate that something will not burn.

Invaluable means that something is priceless. Literally worth so much that it is unable to have a price placed on it. The *Mona Lisa* is invaluable.

Intimate: As a transitive verb *intimate* means to announce or hint. As an adjective or adverb, it refers to close association, as in an intimate friend or intrinsic, essential, close association, friendship, or one's deepest nature.

I did not say, nor did I intimate that.

He is an intimate friend.

Their marriage was an intimate one.

Its/it's: *Its*, without an apostrophe, shows possession or that something is owned, governed, or under the control of someone, some thing, or some group. *It's*, with an apostrophe, is short for "it is" it is a contraction the apostrophe marking the removed letter "i."

That is its name.

It's in the family room.

Lay/lie: *Lay* indicates that something has been placed somewhere. *Lie* indicates that something is reclining or to be situated somewhere.

Lay the tool down.

I will lie on the floor to exercise..

Loose/lose: *Loose* is "not tight." *Lose* means that something cannot be found is misplaced, or that something will be deprived or taken away.

The bolts securing the shaft were loose.

You do not want to lose privileges.

Mass/weight See Mass and Weight.

Media/medium: The word *media* is plural, not singular. Your verb needs to agree.

What do the media have to say about global warming?

What is your favorite art medium?

Oral/ verbal: Spoken communication is *oral. Verbal* means consisting or composed of words. Use oral or written for clarity.

Instructions were oral and given by the teacher.

Written guidelines are better than verbal guidelines.

Plane/plain: *Plane* is an airplane. *Plain* is unadorned or a wide flat expanse.

The SR-71 airplane holds the world speed record.

Buffalo graze on the Great Plains.

The software was plain-Jane (ordinary).

Raise/raze/rise: The verb *raise* means to move something to a higher position. Raze means to tear something down. *Rise* is to ascend or increase the volume or size.

We need to raise the concrete to the second floor.

We need to raze the old building before construction can begin on the new one.

Rise to the occassion.

Sight/site/cite: *Sight* refers to vision, seeing, or viewing something. *Site* is a specific location. *Cite* is to refer to, mention, or reference.

His sight is excellent.

The building site is perfect.

Be sure to cite your sources.

Should/shall: *Should* indicates that something may or may not be done, accomplished, performed, or completed. *Shall* indicates the activity, test, process, or procedure must be performed. When the word *shall* is used there is not doubt, discussion, question, or other opinion. The action must absolutely be performed. Be vary careful with should and shall. They have vastly different meanings. When you are writing for industry, these words must be used carefully and from the knowledge of what their use will require to be accomplished. Their misuse can be, and has been, very expensive. Be very careful when writing procedures or instructions.

You should fill the car with gasoline before leaving on a long trip.

You shall remove the ammunition before cleaning the gun.

Than/then: *Than* is used before or to introduce the second item an a comparison. *Then* indicates time or sequence.

The ship held more people than a small town.

We'll mow the lawn, pick up the clippings, then leave.

Their/there/they're: *Their* is a pronoun showing possession. *There* indicates where something is located. *They're* is a contraction for they are. The apostrophe indicates the omitted letter "a."

Their car is the blue one.

The car is there.

They're coming to dinner (they are).

Your/you're: *Your* means that something belongs to you or you control or govern it. *You're* is a contraction of you are. The apostrophe indicates the omitted "a."

Your home is lovely.

You're late (you are).

You've: This is a contraction for you have.

You've opened a can of worms.

Whose/who's: *Whose* indicates possession. *Who's* is a contraction of who is. The apostrophe indicates the missing "i."

Whose car is that?

Who's there?

Never write "who's time has come." You do not mean "who is time has come."

APPENDIX F

Online Tools

The Associated Press Stylebook
  www.apstylebook.com/

EditPlus Text Editor
  Should you need to make your material HTML-ready, this is a fine editor. We've used many editors and like this one the best.
  www.editplus.com/

Keyword Density.com
  www.keyworddensity.com/

SEO Tools - Keyword Density
  www.seochat.com/seo-tools/keyword-density/

Web CEO
  A dozen SEO tools in one package. *www.webceo.com/*

Webjectives - Keyword Density Analyzer
  www.webjectives.com/keyword.htm

Webmaster tool kit - Keyword Analysis
  www.webmaster-toolkit.com/keyword-analysis-tool.shtml

Word
  Microsoft's word processor. *www.office.microsoft.com/en-us/word/default.aspx.*

WordPerfect
  www.corel.com.

APPENDIX G

HTML Characters and Special Characters

Code to create character	Numerical code	Character	Description
&lsquo;		'	left single quote
&rsquo;		'	right single quote
&sbquo;		,	single low-9 quote
&ldquo;		"	left double quote
&rdquo;		"	right double quote
&bdquo;		„	double low-9 quote
&dagger;		†	dagger
&Dagger;		‡	double dagger
&permil;		‰	per mill sign
&lsaquo;		‹	single left-pointing angle quote
&rsaquo;		›	single right-pointing angle quote
&spades;		♠	black spade suit
&clubs;		♣	black club suit
&hearts;		♥	black heart suit
&diams;		♦	black diamond suit
&oline;		‾	overline, = spacing overscore
&larr;		→	leftward arrow
&uarr;		↑	upward arrow
&rarr;		←	rightward arrow
&darr;		↓	downward arrow
&trade;		™	trademark sign

Code to create character	Numerical code	Character	Description
	&#00; – &#08;		unused
	&#09;		horizontal tab
	&#10;		line feed
	&#11;		unused
	&#32;		space
	&#33;	!	exclamation mark
&quot;	&#34;	"	double quotation mark
	&#35;	#	number sign
	&#36;	$	dollar sign
	&#37;	%	percent sign
&amp;	&#38;	&	ampersand
	&#39;	'	apostrophe
	&#40;	(	left parenthesis
	&#41;	)	right parenthesis
	&#42;	*	asterisk
	&#43;	+	plus sign
	&#44;	,	comma
	&#45;	-	hyphen
	&#46;	.	period
&frasl;	&#47;	/	slash
	0 – 9		digits 0–9
	&#58;	:	colon
	&#59;	;	semicolon
&lt;	&#60;	<	less-than sign
	&#61;	=	equals sign
&gt;	&#62;	>	greater-than sign
	&#63;	?	question mark
	&#64;	@	at sign
	A – Z		uppercase letters A–Z
	&#91;	[	left square bracket
	&#92;	\	backslash
	&#93;	]	right square bracket
	&#94;	^	caret
	&#95;	_	horizontal bar (underscore)

Code to create character	Numerical code	Character	Description
	&#96;	`	grave accent
	a - z		lowercase letters a-z
	&#123;	{	left curly brace
	|	|	vertical bar
	&#125;	}	right curly brace
	&#126;	~	tilde
	&#127; - •		unused
&ndash;	&#150;	–	en dash
&mdash;	&#151;	—	em dash
	˜ - Ÿ		unused
			nonbreaking space
&iexcl;	&#161;	¡	inverted exclamation
&cent;	&#162;	¢	cent sign
&pound;	&#163;	£	pound sterling
&curren;	&#164;	¤	general currency sign
&yen;	&#165;	¥	yen sign
&brvbar;	¦ or &brkbar;	¦	broken vertical bar
&sect;	&#167;	§	section sign
¨ or ¨	&#168;	¨	umlaut
&copy;	&#169;	©	copyright
&ordf;	&#170;	ª	feminine ordinal
&laquo;	&#171;	«	left angle quote
&not;	&#172;	¬	not sign
&shy;	&#173;		soft hyphen
&reg;	&#174;	®	registered trademark
¯ or &hibar;	&#175;	¯	macron accent
&deg;	&#176;	°	degree sign
&plusmn;	&#177;	±	plus or minus
&sup2;	&#178;	²	superscript two
&sup3;	&#179;	³	superscript three
&acute;	&#180;	´	acute accent
&micro;	&#181;	µ	micro sign
&para;	&#182;	¶	paragraph sign
&middot;	&#183;	·	middle dot

Code to create character	Numerical code	Character	Description
&cedil;	&#184;	¸	cedilla
&sup1;	&#185;	¹	superscript one
&ordm;	&#186;	º	masculine ordinal
&raquo;	&#187;	»	right angle quote
&frac14;	&#188;	¼	one-fourth
&frac12;	&#189;	½	one-half
&frac34;	&#190;	¾	three-fourths
&iquest;	&#191;	¿	inverted question mark
&Agrave;	&#192;	À	uppercase A, grave accent
&Aacute;	&#193;	Á	uppercase A, acute accent
&Acirc;	&#194;	Â	uppercase A, circumflex accent
&Atilde;	&#195;	Ã	uppercase A, tilde
&Auml;	&#196;	Ä	uppercase A, umlaut
&Aring;	&#197;	Å	uppercase A, ring
&AElig;	&#198;	Æ	uppercase AE
&Ccedil;	&#199;	Ç	uppercase C, cedilla
&Egrave;	&#200;	È	uppercase E, grave accent
&Eacute;	&#201;	É	uppercase E, acute accent
&Ecirc;	&#202;	Ê	uppercase E, circumflex accent
&Euml;	&#203;	Ë	uppercase E, umlaut
&Igrave;	&#204;	Ì	uppercase I, grave accent
&Iacute;	&#205;	Í	uppercase I, acute accent
&Icirc;	&#206;	Î	uppercase I, circumflex accent
&Iuml;	&#207;	Ï	uppercase I, umlaut
&ETH;	&#208;	Ð	uppercase Eth, Icelandic
&Ntilde;	&#209;	Ñ	uppercase N, tilde

Code to create character	Numerical code	Character	Description
&Ograve;	&#210;	Ò	uppercase O, grave accent
&Oacute;	&#211;	Ó	uppercase O, acute accent
&Ocirc;	&#212;	Ô	uppercase O, circumflex accent
&Otilde;	&#213;	Õ	uppercase O, tilde
&Ouml;	&#214;	Ö	uppercase O, umlaut
&times;	&#215;	×	multiplication sign
&Oslash;	&#216;	Ø	uppercase O, slash
&Ugrave;	&#217;	Ù	uppercase U, grave accent
&Uacute;	&#218;	Ú	uppercase U, acute accent
&Ucirc;	&#219;	Û	uppercase U, circumflex accent
&Uuml;	&#220;	Ü	uppercase U, umlaut
&Yacute;	&#221;	Ý	uppercase Y, acute accent
&THORN;	&#222;	Þ	uppercase THORN, Icelandic
&szlig;	&#223;	ß	lowercase sharps, German
&agrave;	&#224;	à	lowercase a, grave accent
&aacute;	&#225;	á	lowercase a, acute accent
&acirc;	&#226;	â	lowercase a, circumflex accent
&atilde;	&#227;	ã	lowercase a, tilde
&auml;	&#228;	ä	lowercase a, umlaut
&aring;	&#229;	å	lowercase a, ring
&aelig;	&#230;	æ	lowercase ae
&ccedil;	&#231;	ç	lowercase c, cedilla
&egrave;	&#232;	è	lowercase e, grave accent

Code to create character	Numerical code	Character	Description
&eacute;	&#233;	é	lowercase e, acute accent
&ecirc;	&#234;	é	lowercase e, circumflex accent
&euml;	&#235;	ë	lowercase e, umlaut
&igrave;	&#236;	ì	lowercase i, grave accent
&iacute;	&#237;	í	lowercase i, acute accent
&icirc;	&#238;	î	lowercase i, circumflex accent
&iuml;	&#239;	ï	lowercase i, umlaut
&eth;	&#240;	ð	lowercase eth, Icelandic
&ntilde;	&#241;	ñ	lowercase n, tilde
&ograve;	&#242;	ò	lowercase o, grave accent
&oacute;	&#243;	ó	lowercase o, acute accent
&ocirc;	&#244;	ô	lowercase o, circumflex accent
&otilde;	&#245;	õ	lowercase o, tilde
&ouml;	&#246;	ö	lowercase o, umlaut
&divide;	&#247;	÷	division sign
&oslash;	&#248;	ø	lowercase o, slash
&ugrave;	&#249;	ù	lowercase u, grave accent
&uacute;	&#250;	ú	lowercase u, acute accent
&ucirc;	&#251;	û	lowercase u, circumflex accent
&uuml;	&#252;	ü	lowercase u, umlaut
&yacute;	&#253;	ý	lowercase y, acute accent
&thorn;	&#254;	þ	lowercase thorn, Icelandic
&yuml;	&#255;	ÿ	lowercase y, umlaut

APPENDIX H

Unspammable E-mail Code

E-mail is the killer application on the Net. Its use had become ubiquitous. We thought it would be helpful for you to be able to design e-mail links so that they are not "spammable." By that we mean that bad guys troll the Net and pick up e-mail addresses from Web sites. Then, they add these e-mail addresses to their database and you get spammed. Following you will find an unspammable technique for adding e-mail to a Web site. And a spammable, but easier way to add an e-mail link.

The non-spammable method uses javascript and hides your e-mail address by breaking it into several parts. Here we also show you how to include text in the subject line of the e-mail and how to add text to the body of an e-mail as well. Note that the subject area begins with a question mark (?) and the body text begins with an ampersand (&).

Non Spammable:

```
<script language="JavaScript">
<!—
var name = "bob";
var domain = "email.com";
var subject = "?subject=this text appears in the subject line."
var body ="&body=This text appears in the body of the email."
document.write('<a href=\"mailto:' + name + '@' + domain + subject +
body + '\">');
document.write(name + '@' + domain + '</a>');
// —></script>
```

For an unspammable e-mail address that includes an unspammable cc address use this:

```
<script language="JavaScript"><!—

var name = "bob";

var domain = "email.com";

var subject = "?subject=This text is placed on the Subject line";

var body="&body=This text appears in the body of your email.";

var ccname = "&cc=sam";

var ccdomain = "email.com";

document.write('<a href=\"mailto:'+ name + '@' + domain + subject +
body + ccname + '@' + ccdomain +' \ ">');

document.write(name + '@' + domain + '</a>');

// —></script>
```

Explanation:

var name = "bob";
   Enter your primary e-mail address

var domain = "email.com";
   Enter the .com, .net or other last three characters and the dot of our primary email address here.

var subject = "?subject=This text is placed on the Subject line";
   Enter the text you want displayed in the subject line of your e-mail.

var body="&body=This text appears in the body of your email.";
   Enter the text that you want displayed in the body of the e-mail.

var ccname = "&cc=sam";
   Enter the characters of the cc address here. Do not include the @ symbol.

var ccdomain = "email.com";

In addition to creating an unspammable e-mail and cc, this places text in the subject line of the e-mail and places text into the body as well. This is very effective when you want to know that e-mail is coming from your Web site and to have it include text that you wish to choose.

APPENDIX I

An Almost Foolproof Data Backup Scheme

Here is an industrial-strength backup system that won't let you down. If all your computers fail or your office should burn to the ground, you are protected.

A data backup scheme can make, or break, you and your business. It is the quality of your backup system that you will rely on to get back on your feet should your computers crash or be destroyed in a fire or disaster. This scheme is a good one because it provides defense in depth by using multiple technologies and multiple locations to store your precious data. You will use:

❯ Multiple computer hard drives.

❯ Three CDs/DVDs.

    1. One CD/DVD is backed up daily.

    2. One CD/DVD is backed up weekly and exchanged with the one in the safety deposit box.

    3. One CD/DVD is always in a bank safety deposit box.

❯ An external hard drive.

❯ A USB stick memory.

We have three networked computers in the office at all times. Our data is copied to each machine daily. The external hard drive also contains our data as does the USB stick memory in our main desktop computer. Both of these devices are updated at least twice per day. Then there are the three CDs/DVDs. One is updated daily, one weekly, and the third is kept in a bank safe deposit box. While not current, its existence protects years of work, e-mails, and our address book, which includes an extensive media list that we use to send out press releases. This system protects us from any single computer failure, from multiple computer failures, and from the catastrophic destruction of all our devices, even including the office itself. Should our office burn to the ground, we can retrieve data from the CD/DVD stored in the safe deposit box. This provides in-depth capability to recover from all but the most destructive natural disaster.

To this you can also add online storage. To find one of the many providers of online storage, search for online data storage, or online heard drive. Some providers offer one gigabyte free of charge, others offer 5 gig free of charge. We do not recommend storing confidential material online, because, while your online storage may be secure, the connection that you move the data across may not be. We define security for data in the same way we define security for money and financial transactions. So, before you move sensitive material over the Internet, verify that your connection is secure. There can be many computers between yours and the server where your data will reside. Just like with email, data can be read at any one of them as it moves across the net. The time to check the security of your sensitive material is before you store it, so check all aspects of your system, including the security of any pathway that you move data across.

APPENDIX J

Site Search With Google

Google can be used to search your site. This offers a very cheap way to add search capability to any Web page. Simply copy and add the code that follows to the page on which you want the search capability to appear.

1. For this to function properly the site you want to search must be in Google's Database.

2. Change www.webcontentrx.com to the site address you want to search.

```
<FORM method=GET action="http://www.google.com/search">

<A HREF="http://www.google.com/">

<IMG SRC="http://www.google.com/logos/Logo_40wht.gif"

border="0" ALT="Google"></A>

<INPUT TYPE=text name=q size=31 maxlength=255 value="">

<INPUT type=submit name=btnG VALUE="Google Search">

<font size=-1>

<input type=hidden name=domains value="www.google.com">

<br>

<input type=radio name=sitesearch value="">  The
Web<BR>

<input type=radio name=sitesearch
value="www.webcontentrx.com"checked>  Web
Content RX.com</font>

</FORM>
```

Recommended Reading

Beckwith, Harry, and Christine Clifford Beckwith. *You, Inc. The Art of Selling Yourself.* New York: Warner Business Books, 2007.

Bly, Bob. *The Online Copywriter's Handbook.* New York: McGraw-Hill, 2002.

——. *The Six Figure Consultant.* Chicago: Upstart Publishing Company, 1998.

Brown, Paul B., and Allison Davis. *Your Attention Please.* Avon, Mass.: Adams Media, 2006.

Castro, Elizabeth. *HTML For The World Wide Web.* Berkeley, Calif.: Peachpit Press, 2003.

Feininger, Andreas. *Principles of Composition in Photography.* Garden City, N.Y.: Amphoto, 1979.

Heath, Chip, and Dan Heath. *Made to Stick.* New York: Random House, 2007.

Hopkins, Claude C. *Scientific Advertising.* Filiquarian Publishing, LLC, 2007.

Kent, Peter. *Search Engine Optimization for Dummies.* Hoboken, N.J.: Wiley Publishing, Inc., 2004.

Luntz, Frank. *Words That Work.* New York: Hyperion, 2007.

Moran, Mike, and Bill Hunt. *Search Engine Marketing, Inc.* Upper Saddle River, N. J.: Pearson plc publishing as IBM Press, 2006.

Reep, Diana. *Technical Writing Principles, Strategies, and Readings.* New York: Longman Publishers, 2003.

Schwab, Victor O. *How To Write A Good Advertisement.* Hollywood, Calif.: Melvin Powers Wilshire Book Company, 1962.

Stein, Sol. *Stein on Writing.* New York: St. Martin's Press, 1995.

Strunk Jr., William, and E. B. White. *The Elements of Style.* Hoboken, N. J.: Pearson Publishing, 1979.

Veloso, Maria. *Web Copy That Sells The Revolutionary Formula for Creating Killer Copy Every Time.* New York: AMACOM, 2005.

Williams, Roy. *Secret Formulas of the Wizard of Ads.* Austin, Texas: Bard Press, 1999.

Index

About the Author

WAYNE A. ENGLISH is a locally, nationally, and internationally published consultant specializing in online and offline business communications and Web development and technology. Whether a media release, search engine optimization, Web site marketing, e-mail marketing, a newsletter, print or online articles, PDF files, Web development, Web content, or digital photography, WebContentRx.com (that's our corporate name, our Web site, and the title of this book—and not by accident either) we cover all the bases in your communications needs so you don't have to.

This book, like the corporation, is based on our need to pass on knowledge, not simply information. In short, on how to deliver the message, your message, to the ears, eyes, and mind of the most important person in the world: your customer.

Wayne is published in major national magazines, newspapers, tabloids, newsletters, and internationally. The subject matter of these publication ranges from the future of the electric industry to online security, how to search the Web, and sexual harassment. His short dark fiction, *Shift World*, is published online and mirrored at WebContentRx.com.

Wayne develops Web sites, does the keyword research, writes their content, hosts sites, and places everything online to the satisfaction of all concerned. Wayne has taught photography since the late 1970s and still does, but more for fun these days. He also wrote a monthly column for a photography magazine. In photography, as on the Web, Wayne likes working at the intersection of design, art, writing, and technology.

An accomplished instructor, Wayne has taught:

» Software Quality Assurance, which he also helped develop

» The Mathematics, Physics and Metric System sections of a health physics program

» Radiation protection

» Standard first aid, advanced first aid, cardiopulmonary resuscitation

» Volunteer ambulance personnel

» Basic, intermediate and advanced photography, portraiture, scenic photography, lead field trips, and went to India a lead photographer on a scientific expedition. He developed all the photography courses and assisted in the development of other programs he taught as well. You can see his teaching and instructional development background in the section Content That Trains in Chapter 2.

» And, of course, he teaches computer related computer programs.

Occupationally he worked in information technology and nuclear power, and has expert knowledge of electric distribution. The short paragraphs, just a few words really, on the words *should* and *shall* can save an industrial facility thousands of times the cost of this book and materially contribute to surviving an audit. This section is a direct result of his nuclear power experience.